HERNÁNDEZ AND OTERO:
SELECTED POEMS

MIGUEL HERNÁNDEZ
AND
BLAS DE OTERO

Selected Poems

Edited by
Timothy Baland
and
Hardie St. Martin

Translations by
Timothy Baland, Robert Bly,
Hardie St. Martin, and James Wright

BEACON PRESS
Boston

Library of Congress catalog card number: 72–75535

Published simultaneously in hardcover and paperback editions

International Standard Book Numbers: 0–8070–6398–3 (hardcover) and 0–8070–6399–1 (paperback)

Beacon Press books are published under the auspices of the Unitarian Universalist Association

Published simultaneously in Canada by Saunders of Toronto, Ltd.

Hernández Selections:

Copyright © 1972 by Timothy Baland. Some poems and prose pieces contained herein copyright © 1967 by the Sixties Press. Spanish texts copyright 1936, 1937, 1939, 1942, 1952 by Josefina Manresa, widow of Miguel Hernandez.

Grateful acknowledgment is made to the following magazines in which some of these translations have appeared: *The Sixties, Choice, The Nation, The New Republic,* and Barent Gjelsness's *Changes.*

The two photographs of Hernandez and the drawing of the poet on his deathbed are reprinted with the kind permission of Concha Zardoya. Her monograph on Hernandez, published by the Hispanic Institute in 1955, was invaluable in the preparation of this collection. The three-quarter profile drawing of Hernandez was done by the Spanish artist Zamorano.

Otero Selections:

Copyright © 1972 by Hardie St. Martin. Copyright © 1964 by the Sixties Press. Spanish texts copyright 1950, 1951, 1952, 1955, © 1958, © 1959, © 1960, © 1963, © 1964, © 1966, © 1969, © 1970 by Blas de Otero.

For permission to reprint we are indebted to the editors of *The Nation, The Sixties, Poems from the Floating World, Boletin* (instituto de estudios norteamericanos barcelona), and *The Seventies,* in which some of these translations have appeared.

The photograph of Otero was taken by Sabina de la Cruz.

CONTENTS

Selected Poems of Miguel Hernández

v

ZAMORANO

POEMS WRITTEN DURING THE CIVIL WAR:
1936–1939

From VIENTO DEL PUEBLO *and* EL HOMBRE ACECHA

viii

POEMS WRITTEN IN PRISON: 1939–1941

ix

xi

Selected Poems of Blas de Otero

xiii

Selected Poems of
MIGUEL HERNÁNDEZ

INTRODUCTION

I

The spring of 1967 marked the twenty-fifth anniversary of the death of Miguel Hernández. I was in Madrid at the time, and on three occasions traveled to this or that part of the city for an announced Poetry Reading in Honor of Hernández. The first two were suppressed by the government—called off at the last moment.

Finally a reading took place. Twenty-five hundred people jammed a large, tiered classroom in a new building on the University of Madrid campus. People sat elbow to elbow on the bench-type seats. Students clogged the aisles and more people pushed in at the doorway. Others sat down semicircle around the platform that extended out from the blackboard, ringing the desk that served as podium. Many people never made it into the room: hundreds stayed to listen from the lobby.

I remember several bright banners with the phrase: "Homenaje a Miguel Hernández." And a quote from one of Miguel's war poems was centered on the blackboard. It was taken from the poem "El Sudor" ("The Sweat"), where Hernández calls sweat the "brother of the teardrop, first child of the sun." The poem ends:

> with its sword of savory crystals
> and its inundations that move slow,
> sweat will make all of us transparent,
> happy, and equal.

The reading began. One by one ten well-prepared students came to the microphone and read or recited by heart a poem of Hernández. The crowd reacted with intense, thoughtful silence, followed by determined applause, to his sober, unrelenting poems. Other poems of rage and encouragement, written during the Civil War, or poems in praise of the poor people of Spain, were greeted with exuberant clapping and shouts of support from the audience. In one Miguel writes:

> There are no way stations for us,
> except in the heart, or else in the breast.
> To live, a mere bit is enough:
> in a single corner of flesh, you can put up
>   a man.

There was a pause in the reading. A man at the podium now began reading telegrams that had poured in from all over Spain. From Aleixandre and Blas de Otero and dozens of others came messages of support for the reading and statements of affection for Hernández. An uncompromising statement by the gritty Catalan poet, Salvador Espriu, sent the crowd into stormy applause.

Then the reading continued. One by one each reader took his turn. Each had saved his own favorite poem (and most dramatic reading) for this half of the program. War poems predominated, because it is the war poems that embody so unmistakably the solidarity Hernández felt for the suffering of Spain. The same poems now serve as a special link back to Miguel for another generation that has had to grow up in Spain's climate of oppression. Franco's "Thirty Years of Peace" for miners and field workers have been thirty years of misery. A young woman read last. She had her poem down by heart, and in a determined, elegiac reading brought the "Homenaje" to an end with a poem of absence, loss, and uprising. For a split second there was silence. Then long, fierce applause.

II

Miguel Hernández was born in 1910. He died in the spring of 1942, killed by tuberculosis and three years in Franco's prisons. He was not yet thirty-two.

As Neruda tells in the interview about Hernández, Miguel was a shepherd boy from Orihuela, a village in eastern Spain. He educated himself. His first poems were published in local newspapers, and in January 1933, when he was twenty-two, Miguel's first volume of poems came out with the help and guidance of Ramón Sijé. He called it *Perito en lunas* (*Skilled with Moons*). Into the close-knit stanzas used in Spain's Golden Age three hundred years before, Hernández poured the energy of his own twentieth-century childhood, and formed a book anchored in the quiet strength Lorca spoke of in his letter to Hernández, which appears here on page 32.

Three years later—Hernández had by now moved to Madrid—a press run by the poet Manuel Altolaguirre published Hernández's second book: *El rayo que no cesa* (*The Lightning That Never Stops*). Except for three or four longer poems, including the elegy for his friend Ramón Sijé, the book consists mainly of sonnets: sonnets that thrash with the black wings of love, sonnets in which blacksmiths storm and breasts pierce like beaks. Hernández does not deal in pale emotions; his sonnets are about explosions of the heart. A single stanza of Hernández might house stalactites, anvils, or icy archangels. *El rayo* is a book possessed, full of fiery longing and a "touch of homesickness, / half for your body, half for the grave."

That book was published early in 1936. By August,

5

Franco had attacked from the south, and Spain's Civil War was on. Hernández volunteered immediately, and served at the front with the Republican Army's 5th Regiment. Later he was transferred to Madrid to help in the defense of the capital.

In the first month of fighting, the father of Miguel's sweetheart, Josefina Manresa, was killed at the front, fighting on the Francoist side. Hernández voluntarily took upon himself the support of the family, which included the widow, three young daughters, and a teen-age son. It was an act of pure generosity, for Hernández and Josefina were not married yet, and Miguel was hopelessly broke. Poor, and separated by the war (he was in Madrid, she in Orihuela), Miguel and Josefina were not able to be married until March 1937.

Moreover, Josefina's father was a member of the Guardia Civil—that same "elite" group of mounted (now motorcycled) police that shot Lorca and had already detained Hernández once for questioning. Later on, it was the Guardia Civil that arrested him and put him in prison. But Hernández was not a complainer, and toward Josefina's family he felt only affection.

All this time, Hernández was writing poems like a whirlwind: several were printed on postcards and circulated in the army. *Viento del pueblo* (*Wind from the People*), his first book of war poems, came out in 1937. Strong, passionate, and masculine, these poems embody the feeling of common humanity and struggle that linked all classes on the Republican side.

Between 1937–1939, Miguel put together *El hombre acecha* (*The Man Hunts*). In each poem in this book the war hits home deeper. Hernández writes about love-letters without owners, about railroad boxcars full of the wounded.

He writes "thinking of freedom." Sober and brooding, the book details the grief and tragedy of Spain. Two centuries after Goya, Miguel Hernández etched once again the disasters of war in poems bordered with the dark color of blood and silenced longings.

At the end of March 1939, Francoist forces took Madrid. About the same time, a Republican front was collapsing near Seville. Hernández tried once to cross into Portugal; his papers out of order, he was turned back at the border. On May 11 he was captured. The rest of his life—three years—he lived in prison. In less than a year he came down with the illness that led to tuberculosis. After one operation in prison, performed by a doctor a friend had brought in, he had to write to his wife, to ask for gauze and cotton for bandages. And at that very time, as he found out later, she and their infant son had nothing to live on but onions.

Despite everything, poems came—not in a torrent as before, but one by one, like drops of alchemized blood. The poems of *Cancionero y romancero de ausencias* (*Songbook and Balladbook of Absences, 1939–1941*), take on the willowy grace and quieter passion of a man facing death. Yet it is tenderness, not despair, that dominates the book. Out of the isolation and joylessness of prison, Hernández created pine cones of poems—compressed, resinous, fragrant: poems that haunt and are able to move, like this stanza from a poem for his son:

> Lark of my house,
> laugh often.
> Your laugh is in your eyes
> the light of the world.
> Laugh so much
> that my soul, hearing you,
> will beat wildly in space.

7

In the ten years he wrote poems, Hernández had already created a poetry of immense range. Yet even with *Cancionero* he was not done. His *Last Poems* (like *Cancionero* and *El hombre acecha*, never published in book form in his lifetime) are filled with something incredibly pure, a kind of light-giving darkness. As always, Hernández wrote from inside of things. He wrote love poems from inside; war poems from the trenches; prison poems when he lived off memory alone. And finally, in *Last Poems*, he gives us poems whose sources "lean more and more into darkness," poems from inside the death mask, from the inner side of the grave.

—*Timothy Baland*

Early Poems
1934-1936

from

El rayo que no cesa
(The Lightning That Never Stops, 1936)

and

Poemas sueltos
(Uncollected Free Verse Poems)

"ME TIRASTE UN LIMÓN"

Me tiraste un limón, y tan amargo
con una mano cálida, y tan pura,
que no menoscabó su arquitectura
y probé su amargura sin embargo.

Con el golpe amarillo, de un letargo
dulce pasó a una ansiosa calentura
mi sangre, que sintió la mordedura
de una punta de seno duro y largo.

Pero al mirarte y verte la sonrisa
que te produjo el limonado hecho,
a mi voraz malicia tan ajena,

se me durmió la sangre en la camisa,
y se volvió el poroso y áureo pecho
una picuda y deslumbrante pena.

"YOU THREW ME A LEMON"

You threw me a lemon, oh it was sour,
with a warm hand, that was so pure
it never damaged the lemon's architecture.
I tasted the sourness anyway.

With that yellow blow, my blood moved
from a gentle laziness into an anguished
fever, for my blood felt the bite
from a long and firm tip of a breast.

Yet glancing at you and seeing the smile
which that lemon-colored event drew from you,
so far from my dishonorable fierceness,

my blood went to sleep in my shirt,
and the soft and golden breast turned
to a baffling pain with a long beak.

Translated by Robert Bly

11

Por desplumar arcángeles glaciales,
la nevada lilial de esbeltos dientes
es condenada al llanto de las fuentes
y al desconsuelo de los manantiales.

Por difundir su alma en los metales,
por dar el fuego al hierro sus orientes,
al dolor de los yunques inclementes
lo arrastran los herreros torrenciales.

Al doloroso trato de la espina,
al fatal desaliento de la rosa
y a la acción corrosiva de la muerte

arrojado me veo, y tanta ruina
no es por otra desgracia ni otra cosa
que por quererte y sólo por quererte.

"FOR PULLING THE FEATHERS FROM ICY ARCHANGELS"

For pulling the feathers from icy archangels
the lily-like snowstorm of slender teeth
is condemned to the weeping of the fountains
and the desolation of the running springs.

For diffusing its soul into metals,
for abandoning the sunrises to the iron,
the stormy blacksmiths drag away the fire
to the anguish of the brutal anvils.

I see myself rushing recklessly toward the painful
retribution of the thorn, to the fatal
discouragement of the rose, and the aciduous

power of death, and so much ruin
is not for any sin or any other thing
except loving you, only for loving you.

Translated by Robert Bly

Mi corazón no puede con la carga
de su amorosa y lóbrega tormenta
y hasta mi lengua eleva la sangrienta
especie clamorosa que lo embarga.

Ya es corazón mi lengua lenta y larga,
mi corazón ya es lengua larga y lenta. . . .
¿Quieres contar sus penas? Anda y cuenta
los dulces granos de la arena amarga.

Mi corazón no puede más de triste:
con el flotante espectro de un ahogado
vuela en la sangre y se hunde sin apoyo.

Y ayer, dentro del tuyo, me escribiste
que de nostalgia tienes inclinado
medio cuerpo hacia mí, medio hacia el hoyo.

"MY HEART CAN'T GO ON ANY LONGER"

My heart can't go on any longer
putting up with its love-mad and murky storm,
and it raises to my tongue the blood-filled
noisy thing that weighs it down.

Now my tongue, slow and long, is a heart,
and my heart is a tongue, long and slow. . . .
You want to count up the pain? Go out and count
the sweet grains of the bitter sand.

My heart can't stand this sadness anymore:
it flies in my blood, along with the floating
ghost of a drowned man, and goes down all alone.

And yesterday, you wrote from your heart
that you have a touch of homesickness—
half for my body, half for the grave.

Translated by Timothy Baland

"TU CORAZÓN, UNA NARANJA HELADA"

Tu corazón, una naranja helada
con un dentro sin luz de dulce miera
y una porosa vista de oro: un fuera
venturas prometiendo a la mirada.

Mi corazón, una febril granada
de agrupado rubor y abierta cera,
que sus tiernos collares te ofreciera
con una obstinación enamorada.

¡Ay, qué acontecimiento de quebranto
ir a tu corazón y hallar un hielo
de irreductible y pavorosa nieve!

Por los alrededores de mi llanto
un pañuelo sediento va de vuelo
con la esperanza de que en él lo abreve.

"YOUR HEART?—IT IS A FROZEN ORANGE"

Your heart?—it is a frozen orange,
inside it has juniper oil but no light
and a porous look like gold: an outside
promising risks to the man who looks.

My heart is a fiery pomegranate,
its scarlets clustered, and its wax opened,
which could offer you its tender beads
with the stubbornness of a man in love.

Yes, what an experience of sorrow it is
to go to your heart and find a frost
made of primitive and terrifying snow!

A thirsty handkerchief flies through the air
along the shores of my weeping,
hoping that he can drink in my tears.

Translated by Robert Bly

"UN CARNÍVORO CUCHILLO"

Un carnívoro cuchillo
de ala dulce y homicida
sostiene un vuelo y un brillo
alrededor de mi vida.

Rayo de metal crispado
fulgentemente caído,
picotea mi costado
y hace en él un triste nido.

Mi sien, florido balcón
de mis edades tempranas,
negra está, y mi corazón,
y mi corazón con canas.

Tal es la mala virtud
del rayo que me rodea,
que voy a mi juventud
como la luna a la aldea.

Recojo con las pestañas
sal del alma y sal del ojo
y flores de telarañas
de mis tristezas recojo.

¿A dónde iré que no vaya
mi perdición a buscar?
Tu destino es de la playa
y mi vocación del mar.

"A KNIFE THAT EATS FLESH"

A knife that eats flesh, and
sports a lovely homicidal wing,
keeps up its flying
and its light around my life.

Lightning bolt like shivering metal
that flashes down suddenly—
it digs into my side
and makes a red nest in there.

My temples, the flowery balcony
of my early ages,
are black; it is my heart—
my heart that's turning gray.

The evil strength of this lightning
all around me is so strong
that I go back to my youth
like the moon toward a village.

With my eyelashes I gather
salt from the soul and salt from the eye
and I gather cobweb
flowers from my grief.

Where can I go so that
I won't find my destruction?
You have a place on the sand,
and I am heading for the sea.

Descansar de esta labor
de huracán, amor o infierno,
no es posible, y el dolor
me hará mi pesar eterno.

Pero al fin podré vencerte,
ave y rayo secular,
corazón, que de la muerte
nadie ha de hacerme dudar.

Sigue, pues, sigue, cuchillo,
volando, hiriendo. Algún día
se pondrá el tiempo amarillo
sobre mi fotografía.

And to rest from this work
of tornadoes, love or hell,
is unthinkable, and the pain
will make the sorrow go on and on.

But finally I will beat you,
bird, endless lightning,
heart, because no one
can shake my belief in death.

Go on then, knife, keep on
flying, giving wounds. One day
time will turn yellow
on top of my photograph.

Translated by Robert Bly

"LA MUERTE, TODA LLENA DE AGUJEROS"

La muerte, toda llena de agujeros
y cuernos de su mismo desenlace,
bajo una piel de toro pisa y pace
un luminoso prado de toreros.

Volcánicos bramidos, humos fieros
de general amor por cuanto nace,
a llamaradas echa mientras hace
morir a los tranquilos ganaderos.

Ya puedes, amorosa fiera hambrienta,
pastar mi corazón, trágica grama,
si te gusta lo amargo de su asunto.

Un amor hacia todo me atormenta
como a ti, y hacia todo se derrama
mi corazón vestido de difunto.

"DEATH"

Death, enclosed in a bull's hide,
entirely full of holes and horn-
thrusts she made herself, stamps
and feeds on the bullfighters' luminous
    practice ground.

Fantastic roars, killing smoke
and flames shoot out with ecstatic love
for whatever is born, while all the time
death makes the tranquil ranchers die.

Go on, you love-mad animal, starved,
graze on my heart, that tragic grass,
if the bitterness of it all gives you pleasure.

Like you, I can't sleep, because I love
too many things, and my heart, dressed
like the dead, overflows toward the universe.

Translated by Timothy Baland

"NO CESARÁ ESTE RAYO QUE ME HABITA"

¿No cesará este rayo que me habita
el corazón de exasperadas fieras
y de fraguas coléricas y herreras
donde el metal más fresco se marchita?

¿No cesará esta terca estalactita
de cultivar sus duras cabelleras
como espadas y rígidas hogueras
hacia mi corazón que muge y grita?

Este rayo ni cesa ni se agota:
de mí mismo tomó su procedencia
y ejercita en mí mismo sus furores.

Esta obstinada piedra de mí brota
y sobre mí dirige la insistencia
de sus lluviosos rayos destructores.

"WILL THIS BEAM OF LIGHT"

Will this beam of light go on forever
installing enraged animals inside me
and forges mad with anger and blacksmiths
where even the most delicate metal soon folds?

Will this tenacious stalactite never stop
nourishing its long hair stiff
as swords or
inside my heart that is bellows and cries out?

This beam of light will go on forever and never stop
because it pulls its power out of me
and sharpens off its madnesses in me.

This obstinate rock pushes its bud out of me
and it aims the insistent power of its lightnings,
deadly and rainy, straight at me.

Translated by Timothy Baland and Robert Bly

ELEGÍA

*En Orihuela, su pueblo y el mío, se me ha muerto
como el rayo Ramón Sijé, con quien tanto quería.*

Yo quiero ser llorando el hortelano
de la tierra que ocupas y estercolas,
compañero del alma, tan temprano.

Alimentando lluvias, caracolas
y órganos mi dolor sin instrumento,
a las desalentadas amapolas

daré tu corazón por alimento.
Tanto dolor se agrupa en mi costado,
que por doler me duele hasta el aliento.

Un manotazo duro, un golpe helado,
un hachazo invisible y homicida,
un empujón brutal te ha derribado.

No hay extensión más grande que mi herida,
lloro me desventura y sus conjuntos
y siento más tu muerte que mi vida.

Ando sobre rastrojos de difuntos,
y sin calor de nadie y sin consuelo
voy de mi corazón a mis asuntos.

Temprano levantó la muerte el vuelo,
temprano madrugó la madrugada,
temprano estás rodando por el suelo.

ELEGY

Like lightning death struck my close friend
Ramón Sijé in our home town of Orihuela.

Ramón, right now I want to be
the mournful friend who tends the ground
you fertilize and lie in, gave too soon.

Since this useless grief of mine
likes the taste of rain, snail shells, the
    organs of the body,
I'll go ahead and feed your heart

to the disheartened poppies.
Grief bunches up between my ribs,
each breath I take is painful.

The hard slap of a hand, an icy fist,
that violent, that fatal, unseen
blow of an ax has cut you down.

There's nothing big enough to stick my hurt in.
I cry anguished tears,
I feel your death more than my life.

I walk across the stubble of the dead:
no warmth, no consolation from a single body.
I leave this heart of mine behind and try to go
    on living.

Death flew away with you too early,
that morning came before it should have,
before your time you are in the ground.

No perdono a la muerte enamorada,
no perdono a la vida desatenta,
no perdono a la tierra ni a la nada.

En mis manos levanto una tormenta
de piedras, rayos y hachas estridentes
sedienta de catástrofes y hambrienta.

Quiero escarbar la tierra con los dientes,
quiero apartar la tierra parte a parte
a dentelladas secas y calientes.

Quiero minar la tierra hasta encontrarte
y besarte la noble calavera
y desamordazarte y regresarte.

Volverás a mi huerto y a mi higuera:
por los altos andamios de las flores
pajareará tu alma colmenera

de angelicales ceras y labores.
Volverás al arrullo de las rejas
de los enamorados labradores.

Alegrarás la sombra de mis cejas,
y tu sangre se irán a cada lado
disputando tu novia y las abejas.

Tu corazón, ya terciopelo ajado,
llama a un campo de almendras espumosas
mi avariciosa voz de enamorado.

Lovesick death will get no forgiveness out of me,
none for this thankless life,
none for the earth, nor for the black nothing.

In these hands of mine a storm made of rocks
is brewing, lightning, vicious axes
dry and starving for catastrophes.

I want to dig up the earth with my teeth,
I want to take dry, fiery bites
pulling it apart bit by bit.

I want to tear up the earth until I find you,
so I can kiss your noble skull,
unbandage your mouth, and bring you back to life.

You will come back to the fig tree in my back yard:
your soul will be at peace there,
high up among the blossoms, gathering

the wax and honey of angelic hives.
You'll come back to words whispered through
grillwork windows by romantic field-hands.

You'll blow away the shadows on my brow,
and your woman and the bees will take
turns claiming your blood as theirs.

Your heart, now only crumpled velvet,
calls from a field of surflike almond trees
to my voice, wanting and full of love.

A las aladas almas de las rosas
del almendro de nata te requiero,
que tenemos que hablar de muchas cosas,
compañero del alma, compañero.

10 de enero de 1936

And I call you to come to the milky
almond blossoms who are souls flying.
I miss you, Ramón. Ramón, we still have
so many things to talk about.

January 10, 1936

Translated by Timothy Baland

ME SOBRA EL CORAZÓN

Hoy estoy sin saber yo no sé cómo,
hoy estoy para penas solamente,
hoy no tengo amistad,
hoy sólo tengo ansias
de arrancarme de cuajo el corazón
y ponerlo debajo de un zapato.

Hoy reverdece aquella espina seca,
hoy es día de llantos en mi reino,
hoy descarga en mi pecho el desaliento
plomo desalentado.

No puedo con mi estrella.
Y me busco la muerte por las manos
mirando con cariño las navajas,
y recuerdo aquel hacha compañera,
y pienso en los más altos campanarios
para un salto mortal serenamente.

Si no fuera ¿por qué? . . . no sé por qué,
mi corazón escribiría una postrera carta,
una carta que llevo allí metida,
haría un tintero de mi corazon,
una fuente de sílabas, de adioses y regalos,
y *ahí te quedas*, al mundo le diría.

Yo nací en mala luna.
Tengo la pena de una sola pena
que vale más que toda la alegría.

I HAVE PLENTY OF HEART

Today I am, I don't know how,
today all I am ready for is suffering,
today I have no friends,
today the only things I have is the desire
to rip out my heart by the roots
and stick it underneath a shoe.

Today that dry thorn is growing strong again,
today is the day of crying in my kingdom,
depression unloads today in my chest
a depressed heavy metal.

Today my destiny is too much for me.
And I'm looking for death down by my hands,
looking at knives with affection,
and I remember that friendly ax,
and all I think about is the tallest steeples
and making a fatal leap serenely.

If it weren't for . . . I don't know what,
my heart would write a suicide note,
a note I carry hidden there,
I would make an inkwell out of my heart,
a fountain of syllables, and good-byes and gifts,
and *you stay here* I'd say to the world.

I was born under a rotten star.
My grief is that I only have one grief
and it weighs more than all the joys together.

Un amor me ha dejado con los brazos caídos
y no puedo tenderlos hacia más.
¿No véis mi boca qué desengañada,
qué inconformes mis ojos?

Cuanto más me contemplo más me aflijo:
cortar este dolor ¿con qué tijeras?

Ayer, mañana, hoy
padeciendo por todo
mi corazón, pecera melancólica,
penal de ruiseñores moribundos.

Me sobra corazón.

Hoy descorazonarme,
yo el más corazonado de los hombres,
y por el más, también el más amargo.

No sé por qué, no sé por qué ni cómo
me perdono la vida cada día.

A love affair has left me with my arms hanging down
and I can't lift them anymore.
Don't you see how disillusioned my mouth is?
How unsatisfied my eyes are?

The more I look inward the more I mourn!
Cut off this pain?—who has the scissors?

Yesterday, tomorrow, today
suffering for everything,
my heart is a sad goldfish bowl,
a pen of dying nightingales.

I have plenty of heart.

Today to rip out my heart,
I who have a bigger heart than anyone,
and having that, I am the bitterest also.

I don't know why, I don't know how or why
I let my life keep on going every day.

Translated by Robert Bly

LETTER FROM LORCA TO HERNÁNDEZ

My dear poet:

I haven't forgotten you. But I'm doing a good bit of living and my pen keeps slipping out of my hand.

I think about you often because I know you're suffering in that circle of literary pigs, and it hurts me to see your energy, so full of sunlight, fenced in and throwing itself against the walls.

But you'll learn that way. You'll learn to keep a grip on yourself in that fierce training life is putting you through. Your book stands deep in silence, like all first books, like my first, which had so much delight and strength. Write, read, study, FIGHT! Don't be vain about your work. Your book is strong, it has many interesting things, and to eyes that can see makes clear *the passion of man*, although, as you say, it doesn't have any more *cojones* than those of most of the established poets. Take it easy. Europe's most beautiful poetry is being written in Spain today. But, at the same time, people are not fair. *Perito en lunas* doesn't deserve that stupid silence. No. It deserves the attention and encouragement and love of good people. You have that and will go on having it because you have the blood of a poet and even when you protest in your letter you show, in the middle of savage things (that I like), the gentleness of your heart, that is so full of pain and light.

I wish you'd get rid of your obsession, that mood of the misunderstood poet, for another more generous, public-minded obsession. Write to me. I want to talk to some friends and see if they'll take an interest in *Perito en lunas*.

Books of poetry, my dear Miguel, catch on very slowly.

I know perfectly well what you are like and I send you
my embrace like a brother, full of affection and friendship.

(Write to me)

—Federico

Lorca wrote this letter in 1933, shortly after the
publication of Hernández' first book, *Perito en lunas*
(*Skilled with Moons*). It is the only known letter from
Lorca to Hernández, and shows the great generosity
that· Lorca felt toward the younger poets. The book
Lorca mentions of his own was not his first book of
poems, but his book of prose sketches, *Impresiones y
paisajes*. The letter was copied by Concha Zardoya
from the original in the house of Josefina Manresa,
the widow of Miguel Hernández. It was published first in
Bulletin Hispanique, July-September 1958.

Translated by Hardie St. Martin

PABLO NERUDA: CONVERSATION ABOUT HERNÁNDEZ

INTERVIEWER: I think you were one of the first editors who published Hernández, in your magazine *Caballo verde por la poesía?*

NERUDA: Yes.

INTERVIEWER: Do you remember when he came to Madrid?

NERUDA: Miguel Hernández was a shepherd boy, a goatherd. The only education he got was from the priest of the village. It was wonderful because that library of the church had the classics—nobody had read the books in that library for centuries! Miguel discovered them and out of the poetry of the Golden Age he made all by himself a really beautiful language, very strong, completely classic. He is a great master of language. Hernández as a boy came to Madrid in 1934 directly to me, from Orihuela, his village. And he was a happy boy. Once when he was walking with me—I said to him that I had never heard a nightingale, because no nightingales exist in my country. You see, it is too cold for nightingales in my country; and then he said, "Oh, you've never heard . . ." and he climbed up a tree and he whistled like a nightingale from very high up. Then he climbed down and ran to another tree and climbed up and made another whistle like a nightingale, a different one.

I printed his poems—not his very first—but those ones that made the revolution in himself. I must note that he had been doing a lot of reading in my *Residencia en la tierra*, which was published just at that time. And that reading changed his stiff composition, his classical composition, and gave him much more freedom. The fear that he had—the ice was broken and then he became freer and freer and he became a wonderful poet. Don't forget that he was only a young man when he died.

INTERVIEWER: Some people defend the Franco regime by saying that Franco did not actually kill Hernández, but rather Hernández died of tuberculosis while in prison. Do you think there is any question that if the Franco regime had wanted to save him, they could have?

NERUDA: Those defenses are all hypocrisies. Everybody knows that the Francoists shot Federico García Lorca. And Franco made a statement once to the effect that Federico was shot in the beginning, when it was all upset and full of disorder—a sort of accident.

But that defense is full of lies. Because even if Lorca had died like that, Franco still had all the time to free Hernández from his prison. A shepherd boy as he was, a man used to living in the open air, how could he live seven years in prison? He got tuberculosis in prison because he was in prison, but his execution was simply carried out by tuberculosis.

INTERVIEWER: Wasn't Dámaso Alonso around at that time? Couldn't Dámaso Alonso have done something to save him?

NERUDA: I didn't know, but I think the writers were much afraid in that moment, because they never did very much. They perhaps helped him, sending him some things, but I don't think the help was to the point.

INTERVIEWER: What was Miguel Hernández like when he spoke in conversation? Did he speak in images as in his poems, or did he speak of practical things?

NERUDA: He was a serious boy, very thoughtful, and he was always—I was always very curious about his relationship with the goats, and then I asked him and he told me many things I had never thought—he had a very keen observation. He told me once about the *cabra*, the she-goat—that when the she-goat was pregnant, he used to put his ear to her belly, and he would hear all the beginning of the milk coming to the udders, and that made a sound that he described to me. So he was full of all these little conversations about his world. He was a wonderful boy.

INTERVIEWER: I know the younger Spanish poets admire Hernández greatly. How do you feel about recent Spanish poetry?

NERUDA: There is a revival of poetry now in Spain. The poetry was all shut up, but there is a new generation of poets, Blas de Otero and many others, that really means very much. It is a great moment of poetry, very much like the moment when Alberti and Aleixandre and all those were working there. They have great vitality and they have a position—civic position—and I think we have to congratulate ourselves and themselves also.

The conversation took place in New York, June 12, 1966.
The interviewer was Robert Bly.

Poems Written During
the Civil War
1936–1939

from

Viento del pueblo
(Wind from the People, 1937)

and

El hombre acecha
(Man Hunts)

CANCIÓN PRIMERA

Se ha retirado el campo
al ver abalanzarse
crispadamente al hombre.

¡Qué abismo entre el olivo
y el hombre se descubre!

El animal que canta:
el animal que puede
llorar y echar raíces,
rememoró sus garras.

Garras que revestía
de suavidad y flores,
pero que, al fin, desnuda
en toda su crueldad.

Crepitan en mis manos.
Aparta de ellas, hijo.
Estoy dispuesto a hundirlas,
dispuesto a proyectarlas,
sobre tu carne leve.

He regresado al tigre.
Aparta o te destrozo.

Hoy el amor es muerte,
y el hombre acecha al hombre.

OPENING POEM

The field has drawn back
when it saw man, muscles
tightened, rush into it.

What an abyss appears
between the olive tree and man!

The animal who sings:
the animal who is able
to weep and to sink roots,
remembered his claws.

Claws that he adorned
with silkiness and flowers
but at last allows to be bare
in all their cruelty.

My claws are snapping on my hands.
Keep away from them, my son.
I am liable to plunge them,
I am liable to thrust them
into your fragile body.

I have turned back into the tiger.
Keep away, or I will destroy you.

Today love is death,
and man is a hunter of man.

Translated by James Wright

EL HERIDO

Para el muro de un hospital
de sangre.

I

Por los campos luchados se extienden los heridos.
Y de aquella extensión de cuerpos luchadores
salta un trigal de chorros calientes, extendidos
en roncos surtidores.

La sangre llueve siempre boca arriba, hacia el cielo.
Y las heridas suenan igual que caracolas,
cuando hay en las heridas celeridad de vuelo,
esencia de las olas.

La sangre huele a mar, sabe a mar y a bodega.
La bodega del mar, del vino bravo, estalla
allí donde el herido palpitante se anega,
y florece y se halla.

Herido estoy, miradme: necesito más vidas.
La que contengo es poco para el gran cometido
de sangre que quisiera perder por las heridas.
Decid quién no fué herido.

Mi vida es una herida de juventud dichosa.
¡Ay de quien no esté herido, de quien jamás se siente
herido por la vida, ni en la vida reposa
herido alegremente!

THE WOUNDED MAN

for the wall of a hospital
in the front lines

I

The wounded stretch out across the battlefields.
And from that stretched field of bodies that fight
a wheat-field of warm fountains springs up and spreads out
into streams with husky voices.

Blood always rains upwards towards the sky.
And the wounds lie there making sounds like seashells,
if inside the wounds there is the swiftness of flight,
essence of waves.

Blood smells like the sea, and tastes like the sea, and the
    wine-cellar.
The wine-cellar of the sea, of rough wine, breaks open
where the wounded man drowns, shuddering,
and he flowers and finds himself where he is.

I am wounded: look at me: I need more lives.
The one I have is too small for the consignment
of blood that I want to lose through wounds.
Tell me who has not been wounded.

My life is a wound with a happy childhood.
Pity the man who is not wounded, who doesn't feel
wounded by life, and never sleeps in life,
joyfully wounded.

Si hasta a los hospitales se va con alegría,
se convierten en huertos de heridas entreabiertas,
de adelfos florecidos ante la cirugía
de ensangrentadas puertas.

II

Para la libertad sangro, lucho, pervivo.
Para la libertad, mis ojos y mis manos,
como un árbol carnal, generoso y cautivo,
doy a los cirujanos.

Para la libertad siento más corazones
que arenas en mi pecho: dan espumas mis venas,
y entro en los hospitales, y entro en los algodones
como en las azucenas.

Para la libertad me desprendo a balazos
de los que han revolcado su estatua por el lodo.
Y me desprendo a golpes de mis pies, de mis brazos,
de mi casa, de todo.

Porque donde unas cuencas vacías amanezcan,
ella pondrá dos piedras de futura mirada
y hará que nuevos brazos y nuevas piernas crezcan
en la carne talada.

Retoñarán aladas de savia sin otoño
reliquias de mi cuerpo que pierdo en cada herida.
Porque soy como el árbol talado, que retoño:
porque aún tengo la vida.

If a man goes toward the hospitals joyfully,
they change into gardens of half-opened wounds,
of flowering oleanders in front of the surgery room
with its bloodstained doors.

II

Thinking of freedom I bleed, struggle, manage to live on.
Thinking of freedom, like a tree of blood
that is generous and imprisoned, I give my eyes and hands
to the surgeons.

Thinking of freedom I feel more hearts than grains of sand
in my chest: my veins give up foam,
and I enter the hospitals and I enter the rolls of gauze
as if they were lilies.

Thinking of freedom I break loose in battle
from those who have rolled her statue through the mud.
And I break loose from my feet, from my arms,
from my house, from everything.

Because where some empty eye-pits dawn,
she will place two stones that see into the future,
and cause new arms and new legs to grow
in the lopped flesh.

Bits of my body I lose in every wound
will sprout once more, sap-filled, autumnless wings.
Because I am like the lopped tree, and I sprout again:
because I still have my life.

Translated by James Wright

18 DE JULIO 1936—18 DE JULIO 1938

Es sangre, no granizo, lo que azota mis sienes.
Son dos años de sangre: son dos inundaciones.
Sangre de acción solar, devoradora vienes,
hasta dejar sin nadie y ahogados los balcones.

Sangre que es el mejor de los mejores bienes.
Sangre que atesoraba para el amor sus dones.
Vedla enturbiando mares, sobrecogiendo trenes,
desalentando toros donde alentó leones.

El tiempo es sangre. El tiempo circula por mis venas.
Y ante el reloj y el alba me siento más que herido,
y oigo un chocar de sangres de todos los tamaños.

Sangre donde se puede bañar la muerte apenas:
fulgor emocionate que no ha palidecido,
porque lo recogieron mis ojos de mil años.

JULY 18, 1936—JULY 18, 1938

It is blood. It is not hail, battering my temples.
It is two years of blood; two enormous bloods.
Blood that acts like the sun, you come devouring,
till all the balconies are left drowned and empty.

Blood that is the best of all riches.
Blood that stored up its gifts for love.
See it stirring up seas, surprising trains,
breaking bulls' spirits as it heartens lions.

Time is blood. Time circulates through my veins.
In the presence of the clock and daybreak, I am more than
    wounded,
and I hear blood colliding, of every shape and size.

Blood where even death could hardly bathe:
moving brilliance of blood that has not grown pale,
because my eyes, a thousand years old, have given it shelter.

Translated by James Wright

49

"SENTADO SOBRE LOS MUERTOS"

Sentado sobre los muertos
que se han callado en dos meses,
beso zapatos vacíos
y empuño rabiosamente
la mano del corazón
y el alma que lo mantiene.

Que mi voz suba a los montes
y baje a la tierra y truene,
eso pide mi garganta
desde ahora y desde siempre.

Acércate a mi clamor,
pueblo de mi misma leche,
árbol que con tus raíces
encarcelado me tienes,
que aquí estoy yo para amarte
y estoy para defenderte
con la sangre y con la boca
como dos fusiles fieles.

Si yo salí de la tierra,
si yo he nacido de un vientre
desdichado y con pobreza,
no fué sino para hacerme
ruiseñor de las desdichas,
eco de la mala suerte,
y cantar y repetir
a quien escucharme debe

"SITTING ON TOP OF CORPSES"

Sitting on top of corpses
fallen silent over the last two months,
I kiss empty shoes
and take hold wildly
of the heart's hand
and the soul that keeps it going.

I want my voice to climb mountains,
descend to earth, and give out thunder:
this is what my throat wants
from now on, and always has.

Come near to my loud voice,
nation of the same mother,
tree whose roots hold
me as in a jail.
I am here to love you,
I am here to fight for you,
with my mouth and blood
as with two faithful rifles.

If I came out of the dirt
and was born from a womb
with no luck and no money,
it was only that I might become
the nightingale of sadness,
an echo chamber for disaster,
that I could sing and keep singing
for the men who ought to hear it

cuanto a penas, cuanto a pobres,
cuanto a tierra se refiere.

Ayer amaneció el pueblo
desnudo y sin qué ponerse,
hambriento y sin qué comer,
y el día de hoy amanece
justamente aborrascado
y sangriento justamente.
En su mano los fusiles
leones quieron volverse
para acabar con las fieras
que lo han sido tantas veces.

Aunque te falten las armas,
pueblo de cien mil poderes,
no desfallezcan tus huesos,
castiga a quien te malhiere
mientras que te queden puños,
uñas, saliva, y te queden
corazón, entrañas, tripas,
cosas de varón y dientes.
Bravo como el viento bravo,
leve como el aire leve,
asesina al que asesina,
aborrece al que aborrece
la paz de tu corazón
y el vientre de tus mujeres.
No te hieran por la espalda,
vive cara a cara y muere
con el pecho ante las balas,
ancho como las paredes.

everything that has to do with suffering,
with poverty, with earth.

Yesterday the people woke
naked, with nothing to pull on,
hungry, with nothing to eat,
and now another day has come
dangerous, as expected,
bloody, as expected.
In their hands, rifles
long to become lions
to finish off the animals
who have been so often animals.

Although you have so few weapons,
nation with a million strengths,
don't let your bones collapse:
as long as you have fists,
fingernails, spit, courage,
insides, guts, balls, and teeth,
attack those who wound us.
Stiff as the stiff wind,
gentle as the gentle air,
kill those who kill,
loathe those who loathe
the peace inside you
and the womb of your women.
Don't let them stab you in the back;
live face to face and die
with your chest open to the bullets
and wide as the walls.

Canto con la voz de luto,
pueblo de mí, por tus héroes:
tus ansias como las mías,
tus desventuras que tienen
del mismo metal el llanto,
las penas del mismo temple,
y de la misma madera
tu pensamiento y mi frente,
tu corazón y mi sangre,
tu dolor y mis laureles.
Antemuro de la nada
esta vida me parece.

Aquí estoy para vivir
mientras el alma me suene,
y aquí estoy para morir,
cuando la hora me llegue,
en los veneros del pueblo
desde ahora y desde siempre.
Varios tragos es la vida
y un solo trago la muerte.

I sing with a griever's voice,
my people, for all your heroes,
your anxieties like mine,
your setbacks whose tears were drawn
from the same metal as mine,
suffering of the same mettle,
your thinking and my brain,
your courage and my blood,
your anguish and my honors,
all made of the same timber.
To me this life is like
a rampart in front of emptiness.

I am here in order to live
as long as my soul is alive,
and I am here to die
when that time comes,
deep in the roots of the nation,
as I will be and always have been.
Life is a lot of hard gulps,
but death is only one.

Translated by Robert Bly

Aquí no se pelea por un buey desmayado,
sino por un caballo que ve pudrir sus crines,
y siente sus galopes debajo de los cascos
pudrirse airadamente.

Limpiad el salivazo que lleva en la mejilla,
y desencadenad el corazón del mundo,
y detened las fauces de las voraces cárceles
donde el sol retrocede.

La libertad se pudre desplumada en la lengua
de quienes son sus siervos más que sus poseedores.
Romped esas cadenas, y las otras que escucho
detrás de esos escalvos.

Esos que sólo buscan abandonar su cárcel,
su rincón, su cadena, no la de los demás.
Y en cuanto lo consiguen, descienden pluma a pluma,
enmohecen, se arrastran.

Son los encadenados por siempre desde siempre.
Ser libre es una cosa que sólo un hombre sabe:
sólo el hombre que advierto dentro de esa mazmorra
como si yo estuviera.

Cierra las puertas, echa la aldaba, carcelero.
Ata duro a ese hombre: no le atarás el alma.
Son muchas llaves, muchos cerrojos, injusticias:
no le atarás el alma.

PRISONS, PART II

No one here fights for an ox without heart,
but for a horse who sees his own mane rotting away,
and feels his galloping rotting angrily
under his hooves.

Wipe away the lather that trails from his jaws
and take the chains off the heart of the world:
plug up the gullets of the greedy jails
where the sun backs away.

Freedom rots, molted on the tongue
of those who are serfs of freedom, not men.
Smash those chains, and the others I hear dragging
behind these slaves.

Those who only want to get out of their own prison,
their corner, their leg cuffs, and forget all the rest.
That done and over, they disintegrate feather by feather,
they start to mildew, they crawl.

They will be in chains forever and ever.
To be free is something only a man understands:
only the man I see locked underground
as if I were there.

Warden, shut the doors, slip in the cross-bar.
Really tie him up: you won't tie his soul.
There are many keys, many locks, many unjust things:
you won't tie his soul.

Cadenas, sí: cadenas de sangre necesita.
Hierros venosos, cálidos, sanguíneos eslabones,
nudos que no rechacen a los nudos siguientes
humanamente atados.

Un hombre aguarda dentro de un pozo sin remedio,
tenso, conmocionado, con la oreja aplicada.
Porque un pueblo ha gritado ¡libertad!, vuela el cielo.
Y las cárceles vuelan.

Chains, yes: chains of blood are what he needs,
hunks of iron with veins, hot arterial links,
blood splices that will not exclude the later splices,
humanly made.

A man waits in a hole, no one to help,
tense, disturbed, his ear to the wall.
Because a people once cried out, Freedom! the heaven flies,
and the prison-cells fly.

Translated by Timothy Baland and Robert Bly

EL SOLDADO Y LA NIEVE

Diciembre ha congelado su aliento de dos filos,
y lo resopla desde los cielos congelados,
como una llama seca desarrollada en hilos,
como una larga ruina que atraca a los soldados.

Nieve donde el caballo que impone sus pisadas
es una soledad de galopante luto.
Nieve de uñas cernidas, de garras derribadas,
de celeste maldad, de desprecio absoluto.

Muerde, tala, traspasa como un tremendo hachazo,
con un hacha de mármol encarnizado y leve.
Desciende, se derrama como un deshecho abrazo
de precipicios y alas, de soledad y nieve.

Esta agresión que parte del centro del invierno,
hambre cruda, cansada de tener hambre y frío,
amenaza al desnudo con un rencor eterno,
blanco, mortal, hambriento, silencioso, sombrío.

Quiere aplacar las fraguas, los odios, las hogueras,
quiere cegar los mares, sepultar los amores:
y va elevando lentas y diáfanas barreras,
estatuas silenciosas y vidrios agresores.

Que se derrame a chorros el corazón de lana
de tantos almacenes y talleres textiles,
para cubrir los cuerpos que queman la mañana
con la voz, la mirada, los pies y los fusiles.

THE SOLDIER AND THE SNOW

December has frozen its double-edged breath
and blows it down from icy heavens,
like a dry fire coming apart in threads,
like a huge ruin that topples on soldiers.

Snow where horses have left their hoof-marks
is a solitude of grief that gallops on.
Snow like split fingernails, or claws badly worn,
like a malice out of heaven or a final contempt.

It bites, prunes, cuts through with the heavy
slash of a bloodshot and pale marble ax.
It comes down, it falls everywhere like some ruined hug
of canyons and wings, solitude and snow.

This violence that splits off from the core of winter,
raw hunger tired of being hungry and cold,
hangs over the naked with an eternal grudge
that is white, speechless, dark, starving and fatal.

It wants to soften down forges, hatred, flames,
it wants to stop up the seas, to get all love buried.
It goes along throwing up huge, gauzy drifts,
hostile hunks of glass, statues that say nothing.

I want the heart made of wool in every shop
and textile factory to flood over and cover
the bodies that ignite the morning
with their looks and yells, boots and rifles.

Ropa para los cuerpos que pueden ir desnudos,
que pueden ir vestidos de escarchas y de hielos:
de piedra enjuta contra los picotazos rudos,
las mordeduras pálidas y los pálidos vuelos.

Ropa para los cuerpos que rechazan callados
los ataques más blancos con los huesos más rojos.
Porque tienen el hueso solar estos soldados,
y porque son hogueras con pisadas, con ojos.

La frialdad se abalanza, la muerte se deshoja,
el clamor que no suena, pero escucho, llueve.
Sobre la nieve blanca, la vida roja y roja
hace la nieve cálida, siembra fuego en la nieve.

Tan decididamente son el cristal de roca
que sólo el fuego, sólo la llama cristaliza,
que atacan con el pómulo nevado, con la boca,
y vuelven cuanto atacan recuerdos de ceniza.

Clothes for corpses that might start out naked,
might start out dressed in frost and ice,
in withered stone that fights off the cruel beaks,
the pale beak thrusts and the pale escapes.

Clothes for corpses that silently fight back
the most snowy attacks with the reddest bones.
Because these soldiers have sun-fired bones,
because they are fires with footprints and eyes.

The cold hunches forward, death loses its leaves.
I can hear the noiseless sound raining down.
Red on the white snow, life turns
the steamy snow red, sows fire in the snow.

Soldiers are so much like rock-crystal
that nothing but fire, flames, gives them shape,
and they attack with cheek-bone half-frozen, their
        mouths open,
and turn everything attacked into memories of ashes.

Translated by Timothy Baland

CARTA

El palomar de las cartas
abre su imposible vuelo
desde las trémulas mesas
donde se apoya el recuerdo,
la gravedad de la ausencia,
el corazón, el silencio.

Oigo un latido de cartas
navegando hacia su centro.
Donde voy, con las mujeres
y con los hombres me encuentro,
malheridos por la ausencia,
desgastados por el tiempo.

Cartas, relaciones, cartas:
tarjetas postales, sueños,
fragmentos de la ternura
proyectados en el cielo,
lanzados de sangre a sangre
y de deseo a deseo.

Aunque bajo la tierra
mi amante cuerpo esté,
escríbeme a la tierra
que yo te escribiré.

En un rincón enmudecen
cartas viejas, sobres viejos,
con el color de la edad
sobre la escritura puesto.

LETTER

The pigeon-house of letters
opens its impossible flight
from the trembling tables
on which memory leans,
the weight of absence,
the heart, the silence.

I hear the wingbeat of letters
sailing toward their center.
Wherever I go I meet
men and women badly
wounded by absence,
wasted by time.

Letters, descriptions, letters,
postcards, dreams,
bits of tenderness
planned in the sky,
sent from blood to blood,
from one longing to another.

Even though my loving body
lies under the earth now,
write to me here on earth
so I can write to you.

Old letters, old envelopes,
grow taciturn in the corner,
and the color of time pressed
down on the writing.

Allí perecen las cartas
llenas de estremecimientos.
Allí agoniza la tinta
y desfallecen los pliegos,
y el papel se agujerea
como un breve cementerio
de las pasiones de antes,
de los amores de luego.

Aunque bajo la tierra
mi amante cuerpo esté,
escríbeme a la tierra
que yo te escribiré.

Cuando te voy a escribir
se emocionan los tinteros:
los negros tinteros fríos
se ponen rojos y trémulos,
y un claro calor humano
sube desde el fondo negro.
Cuando te voy a escribir,
te van a escribir mis huesos:
te escribo con la imborrable
tinta de mi sentimiento.

Allá va mi carta cálida,
paloma forjada al fuego,
con las dos alas plegadas
y la dirección en medio.
Ave que sólo persigue,
para nido y aire y cielo,
carne, manos, ojos tuyos,

The letters slowly perish there
full of tiny shudders.
The ink feels death agony,
the loose sheets begin to fail,
and the paper fills with holes
like a diminutive cemetery
of emotions now gone,
of loves to come later.

Even though my loving body
lies under the earth now,
write to me here on earth
so I can write to you.

When I'm about to write you
even the inkwells get excited:
those black and frozen wells
blush and start quivering,
and a transparent human warmth
rises from the black deeps.
When I start to write you
my bones are ready to do it:
I write you with the permanent
ink of my love.

There goes my warm letter,
a dove forged in the fire,
its two wings folded down
and the address in the center.
A bird that only wants
your body, your hands, your eyes
and the space around your breath

y el espacio de tu aliento.
Y te quedarás desnuda
dentro de tus sentimientos,
sin ropa, para sentirla
del todo contra tu pecho.

Aunque bajo la tierra
mi amante cuerpo esté,
escríbeme a la tierra
que yo te escribiré.

Ayer se quedó una carta
abandonada y sin dueño,
volando sobre los ojos
de alguien que perdió su cuerpo.
Cartas que se quedan vivas
hablando para los muertos:
papel anhelando, humano,
sin ojos que puedan verlo.

Mientras los colmillos crecen,
cada vez más cerca siento
la leve voz de tu carta
igual que un clamor inmenso.
La recibiré dormido,
si no es posible despierto.
Y mis heridas serán
los derramados tinteros,
las bocas estremecidas
de rememorar tus besos,
y con su inaudita voz
han de repetir: *te quiero.*

for a nest and air and heaven.
And you will stay there naked
inside of your emotions,
without clothes, so you can feel
it wholly against your breast.

Even though my loving body
lies under the earth now,
write to me here on earth
so I can write to you.

Yesterday a letter was left
unclaimed, without an owner:
flying over the eyes
of someone who had lost his body.
Letters that stay alive
and talk for the dead:
wistful paper, human,
without eyes to look at it.

As the eye-teeth keep growing,
I feel the gentle voice
of your letter closer each time
like a great shout.
It will come to me asleep
if I can't manage to be awake.
And my wounds will become
the spilt inkwells,
the mouths that quiver,
remembering your kisses,
and they will repeat
in a voice no one has heard: I love you.

Translated by Robert Bly

EL TREN DE LOS HERIDOS

Silencio que naufraga en el silencio
de las bocas cerradas de la noche.
No cesa de callar ni atravesado.
Habla el lenguaje ahogado de los muertos.

Silencio.

Abre caminos de algodón profundo,
amordaza las ruedas, los relojes,
detén la voz del mar, de la paloma:
emociona la noche de los sueños.

Silencio.

El tren lluvioso de la sangre suelta,
el frágil tren de los que se desangran,
el silencioso, el doloroso, el pálido,
el tren callado de los sufrimientos.

Silencio.

Tren de la palidez mortal que asciende:
la palidez reviste las cabezas,
el ¡ay! la voz, el corazón, la tierra,
el corazón de los que malhirieron.

Silencio.

THE TRAIN OF THE WOUNDED

Silence that shipwrecks in the silence
of the closed mouths during the night.
It never stops being silent, even when cut across.
It speaks the drowned tongue of the dead.

Silence.

Open the roads of deep cotton,
muffle the wheels, the clocks,
hold back the voice of the sea, of the pigeon:
stir up the night of dreams.

Silence.

The soaked train of escaping blood,
the frail train of men bleeding to death,
the silent, the painful train, the pale train,
the speechless train of agonies.

Silence.

Train of the deathly pallor that is ascending:
the pallor dresses the heads,
the "ah!", the voice, the heart, the dust,
the heart of those who were badly wounded.

Silence.

Van derramando piernas, brazos, ojos,
van arrojando por el tren pedazos.
Pasan dejando rastros de amargura,
otra vía láctea de estelares miembros.

Silencio.

Ronco tren desmayado, enrojecido:
agoniza el carbón, suspira el humo,
y maternal la máquina suspira,
avanza como un largo desaliento.

Silencio.

Detenerse quisiera bajo un túnel
la larga madre, sollozar tendida.
No hay estaciones donde detenerse,
si no es el hospital, si no es el pecho.

Para vivir, con un pedazo basta:
en un rincón de carne cabe un hombre.
Un dedo sólo, un trozo sólo de ala
alza el vuelo total de todo un cuerpo.

Silencio.

Detened ese tren agonizante
que nunca acaba de cruzar la noche.
Y se queda descalzo hasta el caballo,
y enarena los cascos y el aliento.

They go, spilling legs, arms, eyes,
they go, throwing chunks through the train.
They pass, leaving bitter traces,
a new Milky Way, with their own members for stars.

Silence.

Hoarse train, disheartened, blood-red:
the coal lies in its last agony, the smoke heavily breathes,
and, maternal, the engine sighs,
it moves on, like a long discouragement.

Silence.

The long mother would like to come to a stop
under a tunnel, and lie down weeping.
There are no way stations for us,
except in the hospital, or else in the breast.

To live, a mere bit is enough:
in a single corner of flesh, you can put up a man.
One finger alone, one piece of a wing alone
can lift the whole body into absolute flight.

Silence.

Stop that dying train
that never completes its journey across the night.
Even the dying horse is left without shoes,
and the hooves, and the breath, are buried under the sand.

Translated by James Wright

TAKING OVER THE REAL

We all know that when poets, caught in adverse circumstances, write false and sticky poems, these poems remain outside their truly important work. Miguel Hernández, on the other hand, totally immersed in the events taking place around him, wrote his very best poems then. The timeliness of Miguel Hernández today comes not only from the esthetic qualities of his poetry—those qualities Juan Ramón Jiménez noticed and hailed when Miguel was just beginning—but also from the way in which Miguel incorporates reality into his poems, revolutionizing the concept of poetry even in his own time.

Miguel Hernández has transformed our poetry precisely because he was a poet who always spoke, as the Gospels say, "verily, verily." If today his poetry continues as the dominant influence on the new Spanish poets, it is because he knew how to take over the real. He knew how to take over into his poetry the reality of the moment, which, paradoxically, lasts longer than the "nontemporal" poetry still written by incompetents who turn their backs on the world in which they live. And if the permanence of Miguel's poetry owes itself, as the defenders of the purity and refinement of "Eternal" poetry would say, to the esthetic quality of his work, it is also true that this quality is not merely a result of but rather essential to his way of conceiving poetry, deep in the insides of what is real.

—Gabriel Celaya

Translated by Hardie St. Martin

FIRST IMPRESSION OF
MIGUEL HERNÁNDEZ

It was Pablo Neruda who saw him most clearly. He used to say: "Miguel, with that face of his like a potato just lifted from the earth."

From the earth. . . . If I have ever known a boy with his roots showing, the pain of being pulled up still on them, pulled up at daybreak, it was he. Root, roots, deep sprouts, a framework of them clinging still to the wet earth of the flesh, the sheath of bones, the roots grew out of the flat potato of Miguel's face, and turned his whole earth-body into a tangle of roots. But on the other hand, when he bent forward, without elegance, with a kind of sad animal's sluggish dipping of the head, to join your hand with his, his head always threw off a sound of green leaves covered with flashes of light.

Yes, Miguel came from the earth, natural, like an immense seed that has been scooped out of the ground and placed on the soil. And his poetry never lost this feeling, the sense of a spirit and body that had come from the clay.

> *Me llamo barro aunque Miguel me llame. . . .*
> *My name is clay even if I am named Miguel. . . .*

The sound of a pick and shovel grinding on him, pounding on the rough stone of his bones, but at the same time, woven into it, a song plowers and laborers sing in the fields.

Like so very many Spaniards today, Miguel was of a Catholic turn of mind. Hence, in his prematurely ended work, curiously detached, sometimes coarse and hard, one finds that fluttering preoccupation with death, where matter is always remembered as perishable at any moment. When I met him in Madrid, José Bergamín's little review, *Cruz y Raya*, had just brought out Miguel's religious play, in the manner of Calderon, filled with the power to absorb and with original strength. Shortly afterwards, in 1936, his first book, *El rayo que no cesa* (*The Lightning That Never Stops*), came from Manuel Altolaguirre's printing press. A genuine lightning bolt with the clear, revealing light of a natural, wise poet. Miraculous lightning, for one thought of it in reverse, leaping out of a stone towards the sky, escaping with its light from that earthy being, awkward and dark.

And July 18, 1936, also was like lightning—it uprooted, swayed, and blinded him until it opened his eyes. It was a day of challenge and reply, of attack by the dirtiest and lowest side of Spain against its noblest and most promising side. An eye-opening date. At that moment Miguel saw his roots better than ever, he understood as he never had that he was clay.

And he exchanged his peasant's everyday corduroy trousers for the brave blue overalls of the army volunteer. And so, then, it was to the war, to his life and contact— "bleeding in trenches and hospitals"—with those heroic people, alive and simple as wheat, that Miguel Hernández owed the whole discovery of himself, the complete illumination of his native, true self. He finally tore out of himself, in his *Viento del pueblo* (*Wind from the People*), a crushing landslide of epic and lyric things, poems of head-on clash and follow-through, of gnashing of teeth and pleading cries, rage, weeping, tenderness, care. Everything that was trembling in him was now interwoven with his profound roots.

But now, after having made his voice heard, like a happy beanfield in the wind, after having been imprisoned, beaten, his chest punished until it hemorrhaged through concentration camps and dungeons, once more Miguel, a discouraged Miguel, returned to the earth, to the black, final hole. The hole had not been opened by laboring peasant hands, happy farm hands, alive with peace and night-dew. Slow, cold hands dug it, and stuck him into it; jealous, violent hands who were convinced he was a bad, dead seed, a dry rootstock without sap for growing. But those despicable people didn't know that there are sweeping winds, helpful rains, soils that revive certain roots that seem to be dried up, that there are nourishments for certain soils they thought were already exhausted.

Meanwhile, we must let some serious boy from Miguel's own foothills mourn for him on a reed-flute with such powerful sorrow that all the scattered flocks will turn for the green ground of the day of hope sure to come.

—Rafael Alberti

Translated by Hardie St. Martin

Poems Written in Prison
1939–1941
from
Cancionero y romancero de ausencias
(Songbook and Balladbook of Absences)

"EL CEMENTERIO"

El cementerio está cerca
de donde tú y yo dormimos,
entre nopales azules,
pitas azules y niños
que gritan vívidamente
si un muerto nubla el camino.

De aquí al cementerio, todo
es azul, dorado, límpido.
Cuatro pasos y los muertos.
Cuatro pasos y los vivos.

Límpido, azul y dorado,
se hace allí remoto el hijo.

"THE CEMETERY"

The cemetery lies near
where you and I are sleeping,
among blue prickly-pear,
blue century-plants and children
who cry out with such life
if a dead body throws its shadow on the road.

From here to the cemetery, everything
is blue, golden, clear.
Four steps and the dead.
Four steps and the living.

Clear, blue, and golden
my son, there, seems far away.

Translated by James Wright

"AUNQUE TÚ NO ESTÁS"

Aunque tú no estás, mis ojos
de ti, de todo, están llenos.
No has nacido sólo a un alba,
sólo a un ocaso no he muerto.
El mundo lleno de ti
y nutrido el cementerio
de mí, por todas las cosas,
de los dos por todo el pueblo.
En las calles voy dejando
algo que voy recogiendo:
pedazos de vida mía
perdidos desde muy lejos.
Libre soy en la agonía
y encarcelado me veo
en los radiantes umbrales,
radiantes de nacimientos.
Todo está lleno de mí,
de algo que es tuyo y recuerdo
perdido, pero encontrado
alguna vez, algún tiempo.
Tiempo que se queda atrás
decididamente negro,
indeleblemente rojo,
dorado sobre tu cuerpo.
Todo está lleno de ti,
traspasado de tu pelo:
de algo que no he conseguido
y que busco entre tus huesos.

"YOU ARE GONE NOW"

You are gone now. Still my eyes
are filled with you, with everything.
You were not born for one day by itself,
and this dying doesn't stop with nightfall.
The whole world is full of you,
while the cemetery has enough with me
for all its needs, with
the two of us it has all the people.
Going through streets, I keep dropping
things I'm picking up,
pieces of my life
lost a long way back.
This agony sets me free,
I find myself made prisoner
by doorsteps full of light,
full of the light of childbirth.
I am the one who fills everything,
with something that is yours and lost
in memory, though it comes back
from time to time.
Time lags behind,
unmistakably black,
permanently red,
time turns gold about your body.
You are the one filling everything,
your hair winds through it all:
only there's something just out of reach,
that I grope for among your bones.

Translated by Timothy Baland

"CADA VEZ QUE PASO"

Cada vez que paso
bajo tu ventana,
me azota el aroma
que aún flota en tu casa.

Cada vez que paso
junto al cementerio
me arrastra la fuerza
que aún sopla en tus huesos.

"EACH TIME I PASS"

Each time I pass
under your window
I am struck by the fragrance
that still floats through your house.

Each time I pass
the cemetery
I am pulled back by the strength
that still blows through your bones.

Translated by Hardie St. Martin

"COMO LA HIGUERA JOVEN"

Como la higuera joven
de los barrancos eras.
Y cuando yo pasaba
sonabas en la sierra.

Como la higuera joven
resplandeciente y ciega.

Como la higuera eres.
Como la higuera vieja.
Y paso y me saludan
silencio y hojas secas.

Como la higuera eres
que el rayo envejeciera.

"LIKE A YOUNG FIG TREE"

You were like a young fig tree
in the craggy gorges.
And when I walked by
I heard you in the rocks.

Like the young fig tree
radiant and blind.

You are like a fig tree.
An old fig tree.
I pass by and am greeted
by silence and dry leaves.

You are like a fig tree
made old by lightning.

Translated by Timothy Baland

GUERRA

La vejez de los pueblos.
El corazón sin dueño.
El amor sin objeto.
La hierba, el polvo, el cuervo.
¿Y la juventud?

En el ataúd.

.El árbol solo y seco.
La mujer como un leño
de viudez sobre el lecho.
El odio sin remedio.
¿Y la juventud?

En el ataúd.

WAR

Old age in the towns.
The heart without an owner.
Love without any object.
Grass, dust, crow.
And the young ones?

In the coffins.

The tree alone and dry.
Woman like a stick
of widowhood across the bed.
Hatred there is no cure for.
And the young ones?

In the coffins.

Translated by Hardie St. Martin

GUERRA

Todas las madres del mundo
ocultan el vientre, tiemblan,
y quisieran retirarse
a virginidades ciegas,
al origen solitario
y el pasado sin herencia.
Pálida, sobrecogida
la virginidad se queda.
El mar gime sed y gime
sed de ser agua la tierra.
Alarga la llama el odio
y el clamor cierra las puertas.
Voces como lanzas vibran,
voces como bayonetas.
Bocas como puños vienen,
puños como cascos llegan.
Pechos como muros roncos,
piernas como patas recias.
El corazón se revuelve,
se atorbellina, revienta.
Arroja contra los ojos
súbitas espumas negras.
La sangre enarbola el cuerpo,
precipita la cabeza
y busca un cuerpo, una herida
por donde lanzarse afuera.
La sangre recorre el mundo
enjaulada, insatisfecha.
Las flores se desvanecen

WAR

All the mothers in the world
hide their wombs, tremble,
and wish they could turn back
into blind virginities,
into that solitary beginning,
the past, with nothing before it.
Virginity is left
pale, frightened.
The sea howls thirst and the earth
howls to be water.
Hatred flames out
and the screaming slams doors.
Voices shake like lances,
voices like bayonets.
Mouths step forward like fists,
fists arrive like hooves.
Breasts like hoarse walls,
legs like sinewy paws.
The heart quickens,
storms, blows up.
It throws sudden black spume
into the eye.
Blood thrashes about in the body,
flings the head off,
and searches for another body, a wound
to leap through, outside.
Blood parades through the world,
caged, baffled.
Flowers wither

devoradas por la hierba.
Ansias de matar invaden
el fondo de la azucena.
Acoplarse con metales
todos los cuerpos anhelan:
desposarse, poseerse
de una terrible manera.
Desaparecer: el ansia
general, naciente, reina.
Un fantasma de estandartes,
una bandera quimérica,
un mito de patrias: una
grave ficción de fronteras.
Músicas exasperadas,
duras como botas, huellan
la faz de las esperanzas
y de las entrañas tiernas.
Crepita el alma, la ira.
El llanto relampaguea.
¿Para qué quiero la luz
si tropiezo con tinieblas?
Pasiones como clarines,
coplas, trompas que aconsejan
devorarse ser a ser,
destruirse piedra a piedra.
Relinchos. Retumbos. Truenos.
Salivazos. Besos. Ruedas.
Espuelas. Espadas locas
abren una herida inmensa.

devoured by the grass.
A lust for murder possesses
the secret places of the lily.
Every living body longs to be joined
to a piece of cold metal:
to be married and possessed horribly.
To disappear: a vast anxiety,
spreading, rules everything.
A ghostly procession of banners,
a fantastic flag,
a myth of nations: a
grave fiction of frontiers.
Outraged musics,
tough as boots, scar
the face of every hope
and the tender core.
The soul rages, fury.
Tears burst like lightning.
What do I want with light
if I stumble into darkness?
Passions like horns,
songs, trumpets that urge
the living to eat the living,
to tear themselves down stone by stone.
Whinnies. Reverberations. Thunder.
Slaverings. Kisses. Wheels.
Spurs. Crazy swords
tear open a huge wound.

Después, el silencio, mudo
de algodón, blanco de vendas,
cárdeno de cirugía,
mutilado de tristeza.
El silencio. Y el laurel
en un rincón de osamentas.
Y un tambor enamorado,
como un vientre tenso, suena
detrás del innumberable
muerto que jamás se aleja.

Then silence, mute
as cotton, white as bandages,
scarlet as surgery,
mutilated as sadness.
Silence. And laurel
in a corner among bones.
And a hysterical drum,
a tense womb, beats
behind the innumerable
dead man who never gets past.

Translated by James Wright

"TRISTES GUERRAS"

Tristes guerras
si no es amor la empresa.
Tristes, tristes.

Tristes armas
si no son las palabras.
Tristes, tristes.

Tristes hombres
si no mueren de amores.
Tristes, tristes.

"WARS ARE SAD"

Wars are sad
when love is not the goal.
Sad, sad.

Arms are sad
if they are not words.
Sad, sad.

Men are sad
who do not die for love.
Sad, sad.

Translated by Hardie St. Martin

"LAS GRAMAS, LAS ORTIGAS"

Las gramas, las ortigas
en el otoño avanzan
con una suavidad
y una ternura largas.

El otoño,
un sabor
que separa las cosas,
las aleja y arrastra.

Llueve sobre el tejado
como sobre una caja
mientras la hierba crece
como mi joven ala.

La gramas, las ortigas
nutre una misma savia.

"NETTLES AND WHEATGRASS"

Nettles and wheatgrass
grow in the autumn
with something gentle,
a long tenderness.

Autumn,
pungency
that keeps things apart,
separates and drags them along.

Rain falls on tiled roofs
as on coffins,
and the grass grows
like my infant wing.

Nettles and wheatgrass,
the same source makes both grow.

Translated by Timothy Baland

"TODAS LAS CASAS"

Todas las casas son ojos
que resplandecen y acechan.

Todas las casas son bocas
que escupen, muerden y besan.

Todas las casas son brazos
que se empujan y se estrechan.

De todas las casas salen
soplos de sombra y de selva.

En todas hay un clamor
de sangres insatisfechas.

Y a un grito todas las casas
se asaltan y se despueblan.

Y a un grito todas se aplacan,
y se fecundan, y esperan.

"ALL THE HOUSES ARE EYES"

All the houses are eyes
that gleam and lie in wait.

All the houses are mouths
that kiss and spit and bite.

All the houses are arms
that shove and want more room.

Sighs of darkness and forest
come out of every house.

In all of them there's the sound
of blood that has not lived.

Suddenly a cry and all the houses
turn on each other and empty of people.

Suddenly a cry and all the houses
quiet down, and have children, and wait.

Translated by Timothy Baland

"RUMOROSAS PESTAÑAS"

Rumorosas pestañas
de los cañaverales.
Cayendo sobre el sueño
del hombre hasta dejarle
el pecho apaciguado
y la cabeza suave.

Ahogad la voz del arma,
que no despierte y salte
con el cuchillo de odio
que entre sus dientes late.

Así, dormido, el hombre
toda la tierra vale.

"HUMMING EYELASHES"

Humming eyelashes
of the canefields.
Falling on man's sleepiness
until his breast
is eased
and his head light.

Drown the weapon's voice,
don't let it wake and pounce
with hatred's knife
throbbing between its teeth.

So, sleeping, a man
is worth the whole world.

Translated by Hardie St. Martin

EL ULTIMO RINCÓN

El último y el primero:
rincón para el sol más grande,
sepultura de esta vida
donde tus ojos no caben.
Allí quisiera tenderme
para desenamorarme.
Por el olivo lo quiero,
lo percibo por la calle,
se sume por los rincones
donde se sumen los árboles.
Se ahonda y hace más honda
la intensidad de mi sangre.
Carne de mi movimiento,
huesos de ritmos mortales,
me muero por respirar
sobre vuestros ademanes.
Corazón que entre dos piedras
ansiosas de machacarle,
de tanto querer te ahogas
como un mar entre dos mares.
De tanto querer me ahogo,
y no me es posible ahogarme.
¿Qué hice para que pusieran
a mi vida tanta cárcel?
Tu pelo donde lo negro
ha sufrido las edades
de la negura más firme,
y la más emocionante:
tu secular pelo negro

THE LAST CORNER

The first and the last:
a corner good enough for the greatest sun,
a grave for this life
with no room for your eyes.
I would like to stretch out there
to be rid of love entirely.
I want it down by the olive tree,
I catch sight of it in streets,
it sinks back in corners
where the trees are also sunk.
It roots deeper, it deepens
a wild strength that's in my blood.
Body, acting out each thing I do,
bones, that something fatal beats in,
I am dying so I can breathe down
on everything you do.
Heart, caught between two stones
both mad to crush it,
you are drowning out of love
like a sea between two seas.
I am drowning from too much love,
and I can't manage to drown.
What right do they have to turn
my life into such a prison?
In your hair the long blackness
has lasted through ages
of the hardest
and most passionate blackness:
I move through your black hair

recorro hasta remontarme
a la negrura primera
de tus ojos y tus padres;
al rincón de pelo denso
donde relampagueaste.
Ay, el rincón de tu vientre;
el callejón de tu carne:
el callejón sin salida
donde agonicé una tarde.
La pólvora y el amor
marchan sobre las ciudades
deslumbrando, removiendo
la población de la sangre.
El naranjo sabe a vida
y el olivo a tiempo sabe
y entre el clamor de los dos
mi corazón se debate.
El último y el primero:
náufrago rincón, estanque
de saliva detenida
sobre su amoroso cauce.
Siesta que ha entenebrecido
el sol de las humedades.
Allí quisiera tenderme
para desenamorarme.
Después del amor, la tierra.
Después de la tierra, nadie.

old as aeons till I can pull myself up
to the primitive blackness
of your eyes and your fathers,
to the corner of dense hair
where you flashed light.
Yes, the corner of your womb,
the alley-way of your body,
the blind alley
where I died one afternoon.
Gunpowder and love
march against the cities,
blazing, stirring up
the population of the blood.
The orange tree tastes of life,
the olive tree tastes of time,
caught between their call
my heart can't decide.
The first and the last:
a shipwrecked corner, stagnant
pool of saliva
over its riverbed of love.
Afternoon sleep that has made
the sun of damp places dark.
There I would like to stretch out
and be rid of loving.
After love, we have the earth.
After the earth, nobody.

Translated by Timothy Baland

IN AND OUT OF PRISON

I was in Paris helping Spanish Republicans make arrangements to go into exile in Chile when I heard that Miguel Hernández was in prison. At a P.E.N. club meeting in Paris I talked with María Teresa León (the wife of Rafael Alberti) and with the French poetess Marie-Anne Conméne. María Teresa remembered that Hernández had been a Catholic poet and that he had written a religious play called *Who Has Seen You and Sees You Still*. Marie-Anne immediately started hunting all over Paris for a copy of the play. Finally we found one, which was then given to Cardinal Baudrillart to read, since he spoke Spanish and was a good friend of Franco. By then the Cardinal was entirely blind, but the play was read to him. He was so impressed that he immediately petitioned Franco for Hernández's freedom. That's how Miguel got out of prison.

Then he went over to the Chilean embassy, in order to pick up his visa and leave for Chile. It was a mistake. The Charge d'Affaires then was Carlos Morla Lynch, who denied him asylum. Morla Lynch has narrated the episode in a little booklet entitled "Report to the Chilean Government Regarding Asylum," in which he explains that he denied Hernández asylum because he had written poems insulting to General Franco. From Madrid Miguel wrote me a last letter, in which he explained in his simple way that he hoped to come to my country and become a Chilean citizen. He left Madrid for Orihuela, to look for his wife and baby son. In the station at Orihuela he was again arrested.

—From an article by Pablo Neruda
in the Chilean review, *Ercilla*

Translated by Timothy Baland

108

MIGUEL HERNÁNDEZ: PRISON LETTERS (EXCERPTS FROM THREE LETTERS TO HIS WIFE)

In this place I feel worse off than in Madrid. No one there, not even those who got nothing through the mail, experienced the kind of hunger we have here, and so we never saw there the sort of faces and events and illnesses we see in this place. Our countrymen seem extremely interested in having me notice how mean-hearted they are, and since I fell into their hands I've been experiencing this. The thin-fingered ones will never forgive me for having placed my poetry, all the intelligence I have, and my unselfish heart—two things of course bigger than all of them put together—in the service of the people in a straightforward and open way. They'd prefer me to be an ordinary coward. They haven't succeeded in that yet, and they won't. My son is going to inherit from his father not money, but honor. But not the "honor" gained by lying and playing along with these worst types disguised as the best. . . .

> From an undated letter written toward the end of 1939. Hernandez was then imprisoned in Orihuela, in a seminary especially converted into a prison, after having spent most of the year in prisons in Madrid

For the last several nights the rats have taken to wandering over my body while I sleep. The other night I woke up and had one at the side of my mouth. This morning I caught another one in the sleeve of my pullover, and every day I have to pick their dung out of my hair. Seeing my head full of rat shit, I say to myself: So this is what I'm worth now! Even the rats come and leave dung on the roof of our

109

thoughts. That's what is new in my life: rats. Now I have rats, lice, fleas, bedbugs, mange. . . . The corner I have for a home will soon be a positive zoological garden, or, maybe, a wild animal cage. . . .

Letter written from a Madrid prison,
May 6, 1940

Josefina, the hemorrhaging has stopped. But I have to tell Dr. Barbero that the pus is not draining through the tube he put in; instead, the opening has enlarged and the pus builds up and then runs out on the bed, during a coughing fit sometimes. This is a bother and interfering with my rate of recovery. I want to get away from here as soon as I can. They are trying to cure me by brilliant ideas off and on, and everything is sloppiness and stupidity and couldn't-care-less. Well, love, I do feel better. As soon as I get out of here, the recovery will go like lightning. Kiss our son for me. I love you, Josefina.

Undated letter from the early spring
of 1942. This was the last letter Hernández
wrote

Translated by Timothy Baland

Last Poems Before Death
1941–1942
from
Últimos poemas

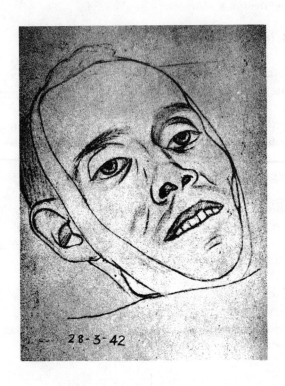

28-3-42

"ENUMDECIDO EL CAMPO, PRESINTIENDO LA LLUVIA"

Enumdecido el campo, presintiendo la lluvia,
reaparece en la tierra su primer abandono.
La alegriá del cielo se desconsuela a veces,
sobre un pastor sediento.

Cuando la lluvia llama se remueven los muertos.
La tierra se hace un hoyo removido, oloroso.
Los árboles exhalan su último olor profundo
dispuestos a morirse.

Bajo la lluvia adquiere la voz de los relojes
la gran edad, la angustia de la postrera hora.
Señalan las heridas visibles y las otras
que sangran hacia adentro.

Todo se hace entrañable, reconcentrado, íntimo.
Como bajo el subsuelo, bajo el signo lluvioso
todo, todo parece desear ahora
la paz definitiva.

Llueve como una sangre transparente, hechizada.
Me siento traspasado por la humedad del suelo
que habrá de sujetarme para siempre a la sombra,
para siempre a la lluvia.

El cielo se desangra pausadamente herido.
El verde intensifica la penumbra en las hojas.
Los troncos y los muertos se oscurecen aún más
por la pasión del agua.

"STILL FIELDS"

Still fields. A feeling of rain.
The earth wild and primitive as it was once before.
Sometimes the joyful sky gets tired of it all
above a thirsty shepherd.

When the rain calls, the dead turn uneasily.
The earth becomes a hole, stirred up, fragrant.
Trees that are ready for death give off
their last deep fragrances.

In the rain the voice of the clocks takes on
the immense age, the agony of the last hour.
They make us aware of the visible wounds, and those others
that bleed internally.

Everything grows deep, concentrated, personal.
Things beneath the rain-sign, as if already deep in the ground,
all seem to want
the final peace.

The rain is like mysterious drops of blood that you can see
    through.
I feel the dampness of the ground go through me,
it would like to keep me in the dark forever,
in the rain forever.

The sky is losing blood slowly out of wounds.
The green deepens the shadows under leaves.
The passion of the water makes the trunks and the bodies
lean more and more into darkness.

Translated by Timothy Baland

113

"SIGO EN LA SOMBRA, LLENO DE LUZ"

Sigo en la sombra, lleno de luz: ¿existe el día?
¿Esto es mi tumba o es mi bóveda materna?
Pasa el latido contra mi piel como una fría
loza que germina caliente, roja, tierna.

Es posible que no haya nacido todavía,
o que haya muerto siempre. La sombra me gobierna.
Si esto es vivir, morir no sé yo qué sería,
ni sé lo que persigo con ansia tan eterna.

Encadenado a un traje, parece que persigo
desnundarme, librarme de aquello que no puede
ser yo y hace turbia y ausente la mirada.

Pero la tela negra, distante, va conmigo
sombra con sombra, contra la sombra hasta que ruede
a la desnuda vida creciente de la nada.

"I GO ON IN THE DARK,
LIT FROM WITHIN"

I go on in the dark, lit from within; does day exist?
Is this my grave, or the womb of my mother?
Something beats against my skin like a cold
stone that starts to grow warm, scarlet, tender.

Maybe I'm still waiting to be born,
or maybe I've been dead all the time. Darkness rules me.
If life is this, I wonder what death would be,
or what I'm getting out of an anxiety this eternal.

Held in chains by these clothes, it looks as if I want
to go naked, to get rid of what can't ever
be me, and makes eyes look troubled and far away.

But the black cloth of mourning, far off, walks with me,
shadow for shadow, toward the darkness, until it rolls
down to the naked life blossoming out of pure nothing.

Translated by Timothy Baland

SEPULTURA DE LA IMAGINACIÓN

Un albañil quería. . . . No le faltaba aliento.
Un albañil quería, piedra tras piedra, muro
tras muro, levantar una imagen al viento
desencadenador en el futuro.

Quería un edificio capaz de lo más leve.
No le faltaba aliento. ¡Cuánto aquel ser quería!
Piedras de plumas, muros de pájaros los mueve
una imaginación al mediodía.

Reía. Trabajaba. Cantaba. De sus brazos,
con un poder más alto que el ala de los truenos,
iban brotando muros lo mismo que aletazos.
Pero los aletazos duran menos.

Al fin, era la piedra su agente. Y la montaña
tiene valor de vuelo si es totalmente activa.
Piedra por piedra es peso y hunde cuanto acompaña
aunque esto sea un mundo de ansia viva.

Un albañil quería. . . . Pero la piedra cobra
su torva densidad brutal en un momento.
Aquel hombre labraba su cárcel. Y en su obra
fueron precipitados él y el viento.

IMAGINATION'S BURIAL

A mason wanted. . . . He wasn't short of spirit.
A mason wanted to build, stone after stone,
wall after wall, an image to the wind
that sets things free into the future.

He wanted a building capable of delicate things.
He wasn't short of spirit, but he wanted so much.
Imagination moves stones like feathers
and walls like birds at broad noon.

He laughed. Worked. Sang. Walls
sprouted like wingbeats from his arms
able to go higher than the thunder's wing.
But wingbeats last a shorter time.

Stone was his go-between at last. A mountain
in full action is worth its weight in flight.
It is weight, stone after stone, and sinks any
thing it stays with, even a world alive with longings.

A mason wanted. . . . But stone makes you pay
for its strict brutal thickness, in a flash.
That man was working on his prison.
He and the wind had rushed their work.

Translated by Hardie St. Martin

VALS DE LOS ENAMORADOS Y
UNIDOS HASTA SIEMPRE

No salieron jamás
del vergel del abrazo.
Y ante el rojo rosal
de los besos rodaron.
Huracanes quisieron
con rencor separarlos.
Y las hachas tajantes,
y los rígidos rayos.

Aumentaron la tierra
de las pálidas manos.
Precipicios midieron,
por el viento impulsados
entre bocas deshechas.
Recorrieron naufragios,
cada vez más profundos
en sus cuerpos sus brazos.

Perseguidos, hundidos
por un gran desamparo
de recuerdos y lunas,
de noviembres y marzos,
aventados se vieron
como polvo liviano:
aventados se vieron,
pero siempre abrazados.

*(Escrita en la Prisión de
Conde de Toreno, a fines de
1939, para el álbum de un amigo.)*

118

WALTZ POEM OF THOSE IN LOVE
AND INSEPARABLE FOREVER

They never left
the walled garden of their arms.
They wound in circles
about the red rosebush of the lips.
Storms tried to part them
out of pure spite;
so did hard-bitten axes
and bony lightning.

They added something good
to a land of pale hands.
Their bodies measured cliffs
being shoved along by wind
between crumbling mouths.
They rummaged through shipwreck after shipwreck,
their arms each time
growing deeper into their bodies.

Hunted down, crushed,
left alone and abandoned
by moons and memories,
Marches and Novembers,
they saw themselves whirled
like dust that counts for nothing:
they saw themselves whirled,
but they have each other's arms forever.

> (*Written in Count of Toreno*
> *Prison at the end of 1939,*
> *in the album of a friend.*)

Translated by Timothy Baland

ETERNA SOMBRA

Yo que creí que la luz era mía
precipitado en la sombra me veo.
Ascua solar, sideral alegría
ígnea de espuma, de luz, de deseo.

Sangre ligera, redonda, granada:
raudo anhelar sin perfil ni penumbra.
Fuera, la luz en la luz sepultada.
Siento que sólo la sombra me alumbra.

Sólo la sombra. Sin astro. Sin cielo.
Seres. Volúmenes. Cuerpos tangibles
dentro del aire que no tiene vuelo,
dentro del árbol de los imposibles.

Cárdenos ceños, pasiones de luto.
Dientes sedientos de ser colorados.
Oscuridad del rencor absoluto.
Cuerpos lo mismo que pozos cegados.

Falta el espacio. Se ha hundido la risa.
Ya no es posible lanzarse a la altura.
El corazón quiere ser más de prisa
fuerza que ensancha la estrecha negrura.

Carne sin norte que va en oleada
hacia la noche siniestra, baldía.
¿Quién es el rayo de sol que la invada?
Busco. No encuentro ni rastro del día.

ETERNAL DARKNESS

I who was sure the light was mine
see myself thrown down into darkness.
Sun-like cinder, star-like joy,
fiery with sea foam, with light and desire.

Blood that is light, circular, erect:
rough longing with no outline or shadow.
Outside, the light buried inside the light.
I feel only the darkness makes me luminous.

Only the darkness. Without a star. Without sky.
Shapes. Beings. Material bodies
inside the air that is without wings,
inside the tree trunk of impossible things.

Pale frowns, the passions dressed in black.
Teeth that are longing to be red.
The shadowiness of pure revenge.
Bodies that resemble plugged wells.

Too little room. Laughter has gone under.
To fly up to high places is impossible.
The heart wants quickly to become
what breaks open the narrow blackness.

Unguided body that goes like a big wave
toward the night that is ominous and barren.
Who is the ray of sun that storms into it?
I look around. Not a trace of daylight.

Sólo el fulgor de los puños cerrados,
el resplandor de los dientes que acechan.
Dientes y puños de todos los lados.
Más que las manos, los montes se estrechan.

Turbia es la lucha sin sed de mañana.
¡Qué lejanía de opacos latidos!
Soy una cárcel con una ventana
ante una gran soledad de rugidos.

Soy una abierta ventana que escucha,
por donde va tenebrosa la vida.
Pero hay un rayo de sol en la lucha
que siempre deja la sombra vencida.

Only the light reflected from closed fists,
from luminous teeth on the march.
Everywhere I look, fists and teeth.
More than hands, mountains reach out to us.

A fight without thirst for the future is nothing.
What a vast plain of dark heartbeats!
I'm a prison cell with one window,
looking out on a huge solitude of barks.

I'm an open window that listens,
where life goes by, full of shadows.
But fighting there is one ray of sunlight
always that leaves the darkness beaten.

Translated by Timothy Baland and Robert Bly

NANAS DE LA CEBOLLA

(Dedicadas a su hijo, a raíz de recibir una carta de su mujer, en la que le decía que no comía mas que pan y cebolla.)

La cebolla es escarcha
cerrada y pobre.
Escarcha de tus días
y de mis noches.
Hambre y cebolla,
hielo negro y escarcha
grande y redonda.

En la cuna del hambre
mi niño estaba.
Con sangre de cebolla
se amamantaba.
Pero tu sangre,
escarchada de azúcar,
cebolla y hambre.

Una mujer morena
resuelta en luna
se derrama hilo a hilo
sobre la cuna.
Ríete, niño,
que te traigo la luna
cuando es preciso.

LULLABY OF THE ONION

(Lines for his son, after receiving a letter from his wife in which she said that all she had to eat was bread and onions.)

An onion is frost
shut in and poor.
Frost of your days
and of my nights.
Hunger and onion,
black ice and frost
huge and round.

My son is lying now
in the cradle of hunger.
The blood of an onion
is what he lives on.
But it is your blood,
with sugar on it like frost,
onion and hunger.

A dark woman
turned into moonlight
pours herself down thread
by thread over your cradle.
My son, laugh,
because you can swallow the moon
when you want to.

Alondra de mi casa,
ríete mucho.
Es tu risa en tus ojos
la luz del mundo.
Ríete tanto
que mi alma al oírte
bata de espacio.

Tu risa me hace libre,
me pone alas.
Soledades me quita,
cárcel me arranca.
Boca que vuela,
corazón que en tus labios
relampaguea.

Es tu risa la espada
más victoriosa,
vencedor de las flores
y las alondras.
Rival del sol.
Porvenir de mis huesos
y de mi amor.

La carne aleteante,
súbito el párpado,
el vivir como nunca
coloreado.
¡Cuánto jilguero
se remonta, aletea,
desde tu cuerpo!

126

Lark of my house,
laugh often.
Your laugh is in your eyes
the light of the world.
Laugh so much
that my soul, hearing you,
will beat wildly in space.

Your laugh unlocks doors for me,
it gives me wings.
It drives my solitudes off,
pulls away my jail.
Mouth that can fly,
heart that turns to
lightning on your lips.

Your laugh is the sword
that won all the wars,
it defeats the flowers
and the larks,
challenges the sun.
Future of my bones
and of my love.

The body with wings beating,
the eyelash so quick,
life is full of color
as it never was.
How many linnets
climb with wings beating
out of your body!

Desperté de ser niño:
nunca despiertes.
Triste llevo la boca:
ríete siempre.
Siempre en la cuna,
defendiendo la risa
pluma por pluma.

Ser de vuelo tan alto,
tan extendido,
que tu carne es el cielo
recién nacido.
¡Si yo pudiera
remontarme al origen
de tu carrera!

Al octavo mes ríes
con cinco azahares.
Con cinco diminutas
ferocidades.
Con cinco dientes
como cinco jazmines
adolescentes.

Frontera de los besos
serán mañana,
cuando en la dentadura
sientas un arma.
Sientas un fuego
correr dientes abajo
buscando el centro.

I woke up and was an adult:
don't wake up.
My mouth is sad:
you go on laughing.
In your cradle, forever,
defending your laughter
feather by feather.

Your being has a flying range
so high and so wide
that your body is a newly
born sky.
I wish I could climb
back to the starting point
of your travel!

You laugh, eight months old,
with five orange blossoms.
You have five tiny
ferocities.
You have five teeth
like five new
jasmine blossoms.

They will be the frontier
of kisses tomorrow,
when you feel your rows
of teeth are a weapon.
You will feel a flame
run along under your teeth
looking for the center.

Vuela niño en la doble
luna del pecho:
él, triste de cebolla,
tú, satisfecho.
No te derrumbes.
No sepas lo que pasa
ni lo que ocurre.

My son, fly away, into the
two moons of the breast:
the breast, onion-
sad, but you, content.
Stay on your feet.
Stay ignorant of what's happening,
and what is going on.

Translated by Robert Bly

"SONREÍR CON LA ALEGRE TRISTEZA
DEL OLIVO"

Sonreír con la alegre tristeza del olivo,
esperar, no cansarse de esperar la alegría.
Sonriamos, doremos la luz de cada día
en esta alegre y triste vanidad de ser vivo.

Me siento cada día más leve y más cautivo
en toda esta sonrisa tan clara y tan sombría.
Cruzan las tempestades sobre tu boca fría
como sobre la mía que aún es un soplo estivo.

Una sonrisa se alza sobre el abismo: crece
como un abismo trémulo, pero batiente en alas.
Una sonrisa eleva calientemente el vuelo.

Diurna, firme, arriba, no baja, no anochece.
Todo lo desafías, amor: todo lo escalas.
Con sonrisa te fuiste de la tierra y el cielo.

"TO SMILE WITH THE JOYFUL SADNESS
OF THE OLIVE TREE"

To smile with the joyful sadness of the olive tree.
To wait and never stop waiting for joy.
Let us smile, let us make the light every day gold
in this sad and joyful hopelessness of being alive.

Every day I feel myself more able to fly, and more caught up
in this smile, so clear, so full of darkness.
The storms that make their way past your cold mouth
also move past mine; it is a brief summer wind.

A smile rises over the final emptiness: it swells
like an emptiness that quivers, still fluttering its wings.
A smile breaks warmly into flight.

Ordinary, steady, it does not fall, it does not darken.
You defy everything, love: you climb over it all.
With your smile you parted from both heaven and earth.

Translated by Timothy Baland

MIGUEL HERNÁNDEZ:
THOUGHTS ON POETRY

There are poets whose voice fits naturally into a thimble, into three-syllable lines; they are wrong to stretch out in alexandrines. They resemble those rivers with wide beds and no body of water.

*   *   *

Poetry is not a matter of rhyme: it is a matter of courage. It demands rhymes from the beginner and determination from the old hand.

*   *   *

I hate poetic games that are merely cerebral. I want manifestations of the blood and not those of reason, which ruins everything in its attitude of thinking ice.

*   *   *

I am sick of so much pure and minor art. I like the disordered and chaotic confusion of the Bible, where I see spectacular events, disasters, misfortunes, worlds turned over, and I hear outcries and the explosions of blood. I don't care for the tiny voice that goes into an ecstasy at the sight of a poplar, that fires off four little lines and thinks that now everything has been accomplished in poetry.

Enough of the coyness and honeyed affectation of poets who carry on like candy-making nuns, all daintiness and sugared fingertips.

—From an article in El Sol,
reviewing Pablo Neruda's
Residencia en la tierra

The classical poet is one who finds the solution to his life and, therefore, to his work. The romantic, one who solves nothing, neither in his work nor in his life.

*　　*　　*

Lack of modesty is a romantic vice: it means speaking of the most intimate things, of what only belongs to a few loved persons. Publishing griefs, misfortunes, with too much freedom, is lack of foresight in a poet; he doesn't let any image or object alone that comes his way.

Man walks alone in the world, but he generally doesn't know this. The man who is a poet, besides being a man, knows about infinite solitude. From the beginning, the terrible storms of solitude are reserved for him.

*　　*　　*

The poet creates in trance as an angel, in moments of crisis as a man.

*　　*　　*

The lemon tree in my garden is a bigger influence on my work than all the poets together.

*　　*　　*

You will see yourself buried under a grain of dirt, you who are so great.

*　　*　　*

Flesh falls off gradually, bones collapse suddenly.

Translated by Hardie St. Martin

MEETING MIGUEL HERNÁNDEZ

I don't have the letter, which is missing like so many other valued papers, but I remember it perfectly. It was a small sheet of coarse paper and on it some compact lines, written in a round, energetic hand. I don't want to put words into his mouth, but I have a very clear memory of what he said: "I've seen your book *La destrucción o el amor* [*Destruction or Love*] which has just come out. . . . It's impossible for me to buy it. . . . I'd be very grateful if you could let me have a copy. . . . From now on I'll be living in Madrid, where I am now. . . ." And he signed it exactly this way:

Miguel Hernandez
shepherd from Orihuela

From then on he began coming to my place often. At that time Miguel was the author of *Perito en lunas* [*Skilled with Moons*], a book which had been printed in a very limited edition in Murcia two years earlier. The book had made no great stir. What stood out most clearly in the book was the promise of this young craftsman; his eight-line stanzas had been formed under the influence of Góngora. The tricentennial celebration of Góngora's death had just ended, and its final waves had reached Hernández's young and vigorous intelligence.

He no longer spoke of *Perito en lunas* now. During those days he seemed like some spring energy closely linked to spring: April, May, June. A country spring. Then with summer almost on us, as the trees were leafing and the sky made the air incredibly brilliant, as nature seemed about to overwhelm the city, Miguel seemed more than ever himself. He too, moving as the seasons moved, seemed to arrive along with that wave of true things that first gave its green to Madrid, then added other colors on.

During that time something about him made him look as if he just came from a swim in the river. And there were many days when that actually happened. My house was on the edge of town. "Where have you been, Miguel?" "In the river!" he answered, his voice fresh. And there he was, just emerged from the river, laughing, his white teeth shining, his tanned and serious face, his hair cut short, one lick of hair over his forehead.

He wore rope-soled shoes then, not only because of his poverty, but also because they were what his feet had been accustomed to since childhood; he brought them out as soon as the Madrid weather permitted. He would arrive in shirt-sleeves, without tie or collar, virtually still wet from his plunge in the river. Blue eyes like two transparent stones over which water had been passing for years glittered in his earth-like face, made of pure clay; there the tremendous whiteness of his teeth clashed like leaping sea foam with dark brown soil.

His head—he had cut off the hair others hoarded— was round, and his short hair had a steely luster; there was energy in the twisted cowlick on his forehead; his strong temples supported that impression, though it was contra-dicted again by the open space between the eyebrows, as if he wanted to turn an honest look on everyone he came in contact with.

Sometimes he and Pablo [Neruda] and Delia [Neruda's wife] and I used to go out to the neighborhood woods of Moncloa Park; on the way back, while we were still inside the park, someone would say: "Where is Miguel?" We might hear him answer us and there he was, lying on his stomach beside a small stream, drinking. Or else he would call to us from a tree into which he had climbed, where he raised his coppery arms into the failing light.

He was always on time, with a punctuality we might say came straight from the heart. Whenever someone needed him, at a time of grief or trouble, he would be there, at the right moment. Silent then, he seemed to radiate a will for good; the honest words he spoke, sometimes only a single word, created a brotherly atmosphere, an air of understanding where the person who was disturbed could rest and breathe. Although he was rough on the outside, he possessed the infinite delicate feelings of those whose spirit not only sees a great deal but is kind as well. When he stood on earth he was not like the tree that only gives shade and coolness. His sense of people was even stronger than his relationship to nature, which was such a beautiful thing.

He was trusting and did not expect to be harmed. He believed in men and hoped in them. The light never went out in him, not even at the last moment, the light that, more than anything else, made him die tragically with his eyes open.

—Vicente Aleixandre

Translated by Hardie St. Martin

Selected Poems of
BLAS DE OTERO

Chosen and translated by
HARDIE ST. MARTIN

INTRODUCTION

Blas de Otero was born on March 15, 1916, in Bilbao, the Basque industrial city he says "burned my youth/like an old rag." It stands for everything he hates and loves about Spain, and if it suffers his attacks sometimes, more often he comes back to it with love in poems that place him in China, Russia, Cuba or any of the other places that have drawn him away from his country at various times, or in Madrid where he has been living for the past few years. Otero attended a Jesuit school in his native city before moving to Madrid for his secondary studies. He graduated in Law, which he has never practiced, in Valladolid and then went on to take literature at Madrid University.

When his first poems came out in 1941, Spain was still badly crippled from its Civil War. As Otero has said, "The war left a brutal gaping wound in life and poetry here in Spain. Post-war conditions were in a way even more cruel than the 'private war' we called a civil war. With the exception of Dámaso Alonso and Vicente Aleixandre, our important poets escaped into exile, and there León Felipe, Luis Cernuda and Rafael Alberti wrote some of their best work. And in exile, Juan Ramón Jiménez, Cernuda and León Felipe died. García Lorca had been murdered during the early days of the Civil War, Antonio Machado had died on the southern coast of France, not long after painfully crossing the border at the end of the war, and Miguel Hernández in the Franco jails, in 1942."

How could any Spaniard ignore the physical suffering of the hungry, the homeless, the poor, many without jobs because they had been on the wrong side; or the psychological torture, the uncertainty, the oppression, the injustice? And yet, the Spanish poets who had written their first poems in the thirties closed their eyes to all this and went back to the kind of poems they had been writing when the Civil War came (Miguel Hernández had gone on to a different kind of poetry during the war, but his poems were not being printed). Their poems were modeled on the work of the sixteenth-century poet Garcilaso de la Vega. As José Agustín Goytisolo, a young poet, said in his poem "Los celestiales" ("The Heavenly Ones"), published in 1958,

> Garcilaso was exhumed, carried around on a litter,
>   displayed
> like a relic through villages and little reviews
>   and enthroned in the capital.

However, these elegant poems they were writing to comfort each other seem to have ended up boring them as well as everyone else. Besides, the country continued in the same tragic condition. And so they decided to try something else, to bury the ruins around them under a huge wave of religious poetry, praying God to make things better. Maybe this is a harsh judgment. It would be unfair to say that all these poets were insincere in their religious poems but, with a few exceptions, mainly members of the generation that started coming up after the Civil War—José Luis Hidalgo and Carlos Bousoño come to mind, beside Otero—the religious feeling in their poems seems hollow now.

Otero's religious poetry has not lost its power. For him God was not a dummy he could pin invocations on and shape his poems around. They are angry, desperate poems, the outgrowth of a profound spiritual crisis.

Two main themes intermingle and strain at one another in Otero's first important books, *Fiercely Human Angel* and *Drumroll of Conscience*: the search for God, who is closer to the stern God of the Old Testament (Jehovah is addressed several times) than He is to the charitable God of the New Testament, and the failure to find satisfaction in human and, with it, physical love. The poet can't reach the God whose shadow dominates his life, and falling back on human love doesn't pull him out of his loneliness. Still, if the failure of human love leaves an emptiness, it is a temporal, tangible emptiness that the man may fill with understanding when he comes out of himself later on. And the shadow, the ghost of God, whose attacks and withdrawals are expressed in terms of physical love and violence, drags him towards eternal emptiness, towards death, nothingness, the end of all hope. To save himself from this end, the victim has to kill the god. And in the poem "Final Sound" we find Him knocking on the door of the man's soul with what sounds like a spade. He has come to dig His own grave in the poet's soul, to make His final sound, and the next thing we know, "He lies buried here." Later, in a poem called "En castellano" ("In Plain Words") the poet reminds us of this death:

> Here you have my voice
> raised against the heaven of the absurd gods,
> my voice stoning death's doors
> with songs of truth hard like fists.
>
> He's been dead long. . . . He stinks now.

He can do without god or gods. He has thrown in his lot with other men. The poet has pushed his way through the "landslide of interior worlds" with a new lease on life. In the last poem of *Drumroll of Conscience* he announces:

> I've returned to life with my death on my back,
> hating everything I've written: the ruins
> of the man I was when I didn't speak.

Because in his next book, *I Ask for Peace and the Right to Speak*, he will start talking as a man to other men. Looking back at his two previous books, we find poems like "World" and "Children of the Planet" in which we can see that the poet had slowly been coming out of his solitude into the world. He puts it this way in "Copla" ("Song"):

> Reality calls me with its hand.
> Here is Spain,
> roads with trees and rocks and hope.
>
> Reality says to me:
> Life is like this,
> I am my own
> seed. Give me
> your hand. And let's walk.

"To the Immense Majority," the first poem of *I Ask for Peace and the Right to Speak*, has Otero rejecting the isolationism of his earlier books. He has lost faith in God and found it in man. He believes in man, in peace, in Spain. His poems will speak for peace and for those in the "huge sad prison" of Spain:

> Why talk of this man when there are so many
>   others waiting
> (smothering in Spain) for a bit of light, that's
> all . . .

The poet has taken on the responsibility to speak, not as a hero, only as an honest poet who has suffered like other

Spaniards, and less than so many of them, to speak for those others

> ... who don't write because they don't know, others
> who don't speak because they can't, scared
> or starved to death ...

The voice is quieter now. There is a new freedom of form that's carried much further in his next book, *In Plain Words.* The rhetoric of his earlier poems gives way to a simpler style that is stripped down to a deliberately flat tone at times. The poet is talking, sometimes using the cadence and language of the streets, but he does this in a symbolic (for the great majority) rather than a literal way, controlling popular speech as one more limited element, subjected to the language and the rules of the whole poem. Some of the shorter poems in this book, which has been attacked more for political reasons than for its style, don't quite come off because there is less room for control, making the book seem almost transitional, than there is in its successful longer poems, some of them among Otero's best, in which the poet never loses his personal tone. From here on, Otero adapts a new form to a new content, cultivating in his later books, in his own words, "free verse, that is subjected to more diffuse, but no less decisive, laws than the traditional ones. As far as content is concerned, there is an interplay of different themes in one and the same poem and a fusion of the individual with the collective or historical."

And not only has Otero mastered a new form, he has cut down the distance between literature (form) strictly speaking and life (content), between the poet and the man, without sacrificing his own for a false public voice. In the first poem of his last book, *In the Meantime*, Otero himself tells us how much the poems are the man:

> The history of my books is clearly
> written in my books.
> ... My books flow
> in rhythm with my life. My word
> in rhythm with the years ...
> ... I've come this far: these pages
> in which I spoke with complete freedom
> of everything, of everything at the same time,
> giving freedom
> to thought, imagination
> and the word.

II

Blas de Otero is outwardly a quiet, slow man. His poems are filled with passion and sensuality that you would hardly expect from this intense man with a distracted air. I remember walking slowly with him in Paris for nearly two hours in silence that was louder than all the scrambled traffic-screech and seldom broken. That evening we sat at a sidewalk café with another Spanish poet and a Spanish philologist who was teaching at the Sorbonne, a brilliant man who seemed too enthusiastic about everything in the presence of the softspoken poet. He suggested, insisted almost, that the poet read and talk about his work soon for a group of students and other university people. Otero did not commit himself and I don't believe he carried out this man's request. Otero says his poems with a wonderful concentration in a deep voice, but he doesn't like to talk a great deal about poetry. He puts what he knows about it right into his poems.

Many things happen to words in Otero's poetry. He can surprise with a sudden twist of phrase. For instance, the expected "cogidos de la mano" (holding hands, hand in hand) is made over into "cogidos de la muerte" (holding deaths, death in death). An ordinary piece of furniture "armario de luna" (simply a wardrobe with mirrors on the outside of its doors) is changed by the attachment of another phrase "y de manteles" (and for tablecloths) into a new kind of wardrobe where moonlight as well as linens are kept. The poet sees something with the sharp insight of a child and the thing is familiar and brand-new at once. Otero also makes us look in a fresh way at phrases or lines he borrows from other poets (Quevedo, Machado, Vallejo). In his work each sound looks for the companion that will follow it and once found they cannot exist without each other.

Otero listens to the unusual logic of his imagination and there is a thread of irrationality in many of his poems that attracts us like the dark fierce moments in Blake or Rimbaud. The inexplicable and the clear are inseparable in some of his poems. His poetry has a baroque interior (not cluttered up in his better poems) in contrast to the baroque exterior of Lorca and some of his generation. Immediate impact on the reader seems to have been the poet's early aim but the later poems are stronger in a subtle way. They are freer in form, but the poem's interior is more disciplined.

In my translations I have tried to reach the same effect as the original where I could, without distorting too much, without coming up with double meanings of the wrong kind. The original of each poem is there to throw the best light on itself.

—*Hardie St. Martin*

from

Historias fingidas
y verdaderas
(Imagined and True Stories, 1970)

MANIFIESTO

Un hombre recorre España, caminando o en tren, sale y entra en las aldeas, villas, ciudades, acodándose en el pretil de un puente, atravesando una espaciosa avenida, escuchando la escueta habla del labriego o el tráfago inacorde de las plazas y calles populosas.

Ha visto zaguanes de fresca sombra y arenas de sol donde giraba una capa bermeja y amarilla, ha mirado las estrellas bajas del páramo o las olas fracasadas del arrecife, fingió desentenderse de los hombres y ha penetrado en todas las clases, ideologías, miseria y pugnas de su tiempo.

Ha porfiado contra la fe, la desidia y la falsedad, afincándose más y más en los años incontrovertibles, el esfuerzo renovado y la verdad sin juego. Ha leído hermosas y lamentables páginas, no ha perdonado ni olvidado porque apenas si recordaba, ha dejado que hablen la envidia sin causa y el odio sin pretexto, ha escrito unas pocas líneas ineludibles y ha arrojado el periódico a los perros.

Un hombre recorre su historia y la de su patria y las halló similares, difíciles de explicar y acaso tan sencilla la suya como el sol, que sale para todos.

MANIFESTO

A man travels through Spain, walking or by train, he goes in and out of villages, towns, cities, resting his elbows on the railing of a bridge, crossing a broad avenue, listening to the plain speech of the laborer or the harsh traffic in crowded squares and streets.

He has seen vestibules of cool shade and arenas of sunlight where a bright red and yellow bullfighter's cape swirled, he has watched the low stars on the bleak tableland and the waves stopped dead on the reef, he has pretended not to have anything to do with others but he has found his way into every class, ideology and struggle of his time.

He has fought battles against faith, sloth and insincerity, gradually sinking himself into the implacable years, into constant renewal, into the truth that doesn't play games. He has read beautiful and pathetic pages, he has not forgiven or forgotten, because he hardly remembered, he has let pointless envy and irrational hatred have their say, he has written a few inevitable lines and thrown the newspaper to the dogs.

A man travels through his own history and the history of his country, and he has found them much alike and hard to explain, yet his own may be as simple as the sun that rises for everybody.

ANDAR

Siempre han coexistido durante algún tiempo dos mundos o maneras de andar el hombre tras o detrás de la historia: apuntalando ideas renqueantes; cimentando nuevas bases en que asentar la vida.

Y vi el mundo revuelto de náufragos abrazados; y el mundo recién surgido entre tumbas resquebrajadas e inscripciones falaces.

Salime al campo y vi que el sol bebía la sangre de millones de seres bestialmente sacrificados; y seguí el camino que hallé poblado de pasos que marchaban segura, serenamente.

WALKING

For some time now there have been two worlds or ways for man to walk, behind history or catching up with it: propping up crippled ideas, laying down new foundations on which to set life up.

And I saw the world as a sea churning with people, hanging on to one another as they went down; and the world just risen among broken tombs and inscriptions that lied.

I went out to the countryside and saw the sun drinking the blood of millions of people who had been sacrificed brutally; and I followed the road I found crowded with footsteps that moved along calmly, sure of what was ahead of them.

LIBERTAD

A qué nos referimos cuando escribimos o pronunciamos, cuando luchamos por esta palabra, bien sea con nuestro afán, con nuestro poema, con nuestras armas. Porque hay, que yo entienda, dos rostros de la libertad, excluyo el tercero de los grandes rotativos, los monstruosos monopolios y la altiva y triste estatua. Hubo un hombre, llamado Walt Whitman, que paseó a grandes pasos entre aquellos hombres, ómnibus, instituciones, salió a pecho descubierto a las vastas extensiones de los lagos, las plantaciones y las colinas, osciló su verso como un sendero o una aguja, el destino le libró de este otro tiempo en que se trizan todos los barómetros.

Yo hablo aquí ahora de nuestra libertad interior de personas y exterior de ciudadanos, es la misma y no es la misma, hubo que limitar en exceso la segunda, demasiado la primera, para que no nos comieran con sus trampas, para nivelar la justicia y las posibilidades que parecían imposibles (bonita intervención, ni que fueras procurador o abogado de los mansitos leones).

Sin saber cómo, nuestra íntima libertad queda aislada, a merced de sí misma, reimos o lloramos—*también*—por nuestra ventura o nuestra desgracia intransferibles, y la mayor locura que puede hacer un hombre en esta vida es intentar sacrificar este reducto en aras de una "prosperidad nacional," porque ¿con qué mano va uno a combatir si no disponemos de ella plenamente?

FREEDOM

What do we mean when we write it or say it, when we fight for this word, with energy, with poems, with rifles? For, as I see it, freedom has two faces; I leave out the third, which is the face of the big rotary presses, the monster corporations and the arrogant, sad statue. There was a man named Walt Whitman, who stepped out with decision among those men, trolleys, institutions; he went out exposed to the great stretches of lakes, the plantations and the hills; his poetry wandered like a road or a needle, destiny freed him from this other time in which all the barometers go to pieces.

I am speaking now of our inner freedom as persons and our public freedom as citizens, it's the same and yet not the same, we had to cut back too much on the second, and on the first as well, so that they wouldn't eat us up with their tricks, so that justice would be equal and those opportunities that seemed impossible (a nice intervention, even if you were a counselor or a lawyer for those tame little lions).

Our intimate freedom is cut off, I don't know how, left to its own mercy, we laugh, or cry too, at the good luck or bad that can't be palmed off, and the craziest thing a man can do in this life is to attempt to sacrifice this stronghold on the altar of "national prosperity," for what hand are we going to use to fight with if our hands are tied?

from

Ancia, 1958

LO ETERNO

Un mundo como un árbol desgajado.
Una generación desarraigada.
Unos hombres sin más destino que
apuntalar las ruinas.

          Rompe el mar
en el mar, como un himen inmenso,
mecen los árboles el silencio verde,
las estrellas crepitan, yo las oigo.

Sólo el hombre está solo. Es que se sabe
vivo y mortal. Es que se siente huir
—ese río del tiempo hacia la muerte—.

Es que quiere quedar. Seguir siguiendo,
subir, a contramuerte, hasta lo eterno.
Le da miedo mirar. Cierra los ojos
para dormir el sueño de los vivos.

Pero la muerte, desde dentro, ve.
Pero la muerte, desde dentro, vela.
Pero la muerte, desde dentro, mata.

. . . El mar—la mar—, como un himen inmenso,
los árboles moviendo el verde aire,
la nieve en llamas de la luz en vilo . . .

THE ETERNAL

A world like a mutilated tree.
An uprooted generation.
Men whose single destiny is to prop
ruins.

> *The sea breaks*
on the sea like an enormous hymen,
trees rock the green silence,
the stars crackle, I hear them.

Only man is alone. Because he knows
he is alive and mortal. Because he feels
himself running—river of time towards death—.

Because he wants to stay. To keep going,
to ascend, against death's current, to the eternal.
He is afraid to look. He closes his eyes
to sleep the sleep of those who are alive.

But death sees, from within.
But death waits there, within.
But death strikes, from within.

. . . The sea—the sea—like an enormous hymen,
the trees stirring the green air,
the light suspended like snow on fire.

ENTONCES Y ADEMÁS

Cuando el llanto, partido en dos mitades,
cuelga, sombríamente, de las manos,
y el viento, vengador, viene y va, estira
del corazón, ensancha el desamparo.

Cuando el llanto, tendido como un llanto
silencioso, se arrastra por las calles
solitarias, se enreda entre los pies,
y luego suavemente se deshace.

Cuando morir es ir donde no hay nadie,
nadie, nadie; caer, no llegar nunca,
nunca, nunca; morirse y no poder
hablar, gritar, hacer la gran pregunta.

Cuando besar una mujer desnuda
sabe a ceniza, a bajamar, a broza,
y el abrazo final es esa franja
sucia que deja, en bajamar, la ola.

Entonces, y también cuando se toca
con las dos manos el vacío, el hueco,
y no hay donde apoyarse, no hay columnas
que no sean de sombra y de silencio.

Entonces, y además cuando da miedo
ser hombre, y estar solo es estar solo,
nada más que estar solo, sorprenderse
de ser hombre, ajenarse: ahogarse sólo.

Cuando el llanto, parado ante nosotros . . .

THEN AND EVEN MORE

When your weeping, broken in two pieces,
hangs, full of shadows, from your hands,
and the wind, vengeful, comes and goes, stretches
the heart, swells the sense of abandonment.

When your weeping, stretched out like a silent
weeping, drags itself down solitary
streets, curls around your feet,
and then quietly falls apart again.

When to die is to go where there's no one,
no one, no one; to fall and never get anywhere,
never, never; to die and not be able
to talk, to cry out, to ask the big question.

When kissing a naked woman
tastes of ashes, low tide, rotten leaves,
and the final hug is that scummy fringe
the wave leaves behind at low tide.

Then, and also when you touch emptiness,
the big gap, with both your hands,
and there's nothing to hold on to, there
are only pillars of darkness and silence.

Then, and even more when it's terrifying
to be a man, and to be alone is to be alone,
that's all, just to be alone, astounded
to be a man, displaced: drowning alone.

When your weeping, come to a stop in front of us . . .

HOMBRE

Luchando, cuerpo a cuerpo, con la muerte,
al borde del abismo, estoy clamando
a Dios. Y su silencio, retumbando,
ahoga mi voz en el vacío inerte.

Oh Dios. Si he de morir, quiero tenerte
despierto. Y, noche a noche, no sé cuándo
oirás mi voz. Oh Dios. Estoy hablando
solo. Arañando sombras para verte.

Alzo la mano, y tú me la cercenas.
Abro los ojos: me los sajas vivos.
Sed tengo, y sal se vuelven tus arenas.

Esto es ser hombre: horror a manos llenas.
Ser—y no ser—eternos, fugitivos.
¡Ángel con grandes alas de cadenas!

MAN

Fighting with death, hand to hand,
at the edge of the cliff, I am crying out
to God. And his silence, echoing back,
drowns out my voice in the unmoving emptiness.

My God. If I have to die, I want to have you
while awake. Night after night, I can't tell when
my voice will be heard. God. I am talking
to myself. Ripping shadows aside to see you.

I raise my hand, and you lop it off.
I raise my eyes: you gouge them out alive.
I am thirsty, and your sands turn to salt.

This is what being a man means: terror on all sides.
To be—and not be—eternal, dying.
Angel with enormous wings like chains!

POSTRER RUIDO

Homenaje a Francisco de Quevedo.

Ya escucho a solas, el derrumbamiento
de mundos interiores espantoso;
bate mi vida el viento hombrón, borroso
el claustro ensimismal del pensamiento.

Morir, soñar. . . . Un desvanecimiento
verdadero desvae el alma: acoso
—no sé, acaso—de un ser tan misterioso
como este hombre que yo soy y siento.

A toda luz, el cielo se derrumba,
arriado de raíz, sobre la tumba
donde mi alma vive sepultada.

Tramo a tramo, tremando, se deshace
el cerco de lo eterno. A són de azada
llama Dios en mi alma. Y, aquí yace.

FINAL SOUND

Homage to Francisco de Quevedo.

I'm listening alone to the spine-chilling
landslide of interior worlds;
the brutal wind hammers my life, everything is dim
in the cloister of thought buried in itself.

To die, to dream. . . . If you faint and really fall
it empties out the soul: tracked down
—maybe, I don't know—by someone as
mysterious as this man I am and feel.

In broad daylight the sky collapses,
pulled down to the ground, on top of the tomb
where my soul is buried alive.

Section by section, quivering, the wall
around the eternal disintegrates.
God calls to my soul like a spade ringing.
And here He lies.

A PUNTO DE CAER

Nada es tan necesario al hombre como un trozo de mar
y un margen de esperanza más allá de la muerte,
es todo lo que necesito, y acaso un par de alas
abiertas en el capítulo primero de la carne.

No sé cómo decirlo, con qué cara
cambiarme por un ángel de los de antes de la tierra,
se me han roto los brazos de tanto darles cuerda,
decidme qué haré ahora, decidme qué hora es y si aún hay
    tiempo,
es preciso que suba a cambiarme, que me arrepienta sin
    perder una lágrima,
una sólo, una lágrima huérfana,
por favor, decidme qué hora es la de las lágrimas,
sobre todo la de las lágrimas sin más ni más que llanto
y llanto todavía y para siempre.

Nada es tan necesario al hombre como un par de lágrimas
a punto de caer en la desesperación.

ABOUT TO FALL

A man needs nothing so much as a strip of sea
and a shore of hope on the other side of death,
that's all I need, and maybe a pair of wings
spread open at the opening chapter of the body.

I don't know how to say it, if I have enough gall
to exchange myself for one of those angels that existed
    before the earth,
my arms have broken down from winding them up so often,
tell me what to do now, tell me what time it is and if there's
    still time,
it's time to go up and change, and repent without dropping
    a tear,
not one solitary orphaned tear,
please, tell me what is the right time for tears,
above all for tears that are nothing more nor less than
    weeping,
weeping now and forever.

A man needs nothing so much as a pair of tears
about to fall into despair.

Era deforme como un ángel caído en un patio entre algodones.
Como esas horribles esculturas donde la maternidad da a luz
    a la belleza.
Porque he conocido cosas peores que la desesperación a mis
    treinta y dos años,
y una mujer me acariciaba entre los muslos de las montañas
    llenas de sangre
con una lentitud y una insistencia que hacía gemir a las
    mariposas refugiadas en el bolsillo.

Me acuerdo que una vez estuve a punto de asesinar a mi
    sombra
solamente por una pequeña deformidad que se advertía de-
    bajo de la tetilla izquierda de mi alma.
Pero ya pasó todo, así que afortunadamente el tiempo se
    desliza entre los álamos
y la primavera restalla su gran látigo verde.

Cuando me asalta el recuerdo de lo espantoso que he sido
    conmigo mismo
y de las noches trenzadas alrededor de mi garganta sin una
    pizca de luna para aliviar la sed,
y vienen de golpe años y años pasados en la soledad de las
    aceras públicas,
en el desamparo de las salas de recibir de los médicos,
al borde de los confesonarios,
junto a las faldas frías y las muchachas pálidas de la última
    remesa,
sin tener siquiera un libro a mano donde apoyar descuidada-
    mente la cabeza,

CHAP. 10 BOOK II

I was deformed like an angel fallen among cottons in a
    courtyard.
Like those terrible pieces of sculpture in which maternity
    gives birth to beauty.
Because at thirty-two I have known things worse than
    despair,
and a woman caressed me between the thighs of mountains
    filled with blood
so slowly and insistently that the butterflies sheltered in my
    pocket groaned.

I recall the time I was about to murder my shadow
simply because of a tiny deformity which could be observed
    under the left nipple of my soul.
But everything is over and done with, so that fortunately
    time glides between the poplars
and spring cracks its long green whip.

When I am overcome by the memory of how horribly I have
    treated myself
and of the nights tangled round my throat without a drop
    of moonlight to take care of my thirst,
and all at once years and years spent in the solitude of public
    sidewalks come rushing in,
years spent in the helplessness of doctors' waiting rooms,
on the edge of confessionals,
next to the cold skirts and the newest load of sallow girls
    shipped in,
without even a book handy to serve as makeshift pillow for
    my head

169

ni una pequeña flor ni nada que mereciese la pena de morir
   en aquel instante,
cuando me asaltan estos recuerdos comprendo de repente la
   deformidad de todo, y me resigno a ser ceniza, solitaria
   ceniza húmeda de lágrimas.

or a little flower or anything for which it would be worth
dying at that moment;
when these memories jolt me, I suddenly realize how hideous
everything is and I resign myself to being ashes, lonely
ashes damp with tears.

EL CLAUSTRO DE LAS SOMBRAS

. . . to the antique order of the dead
—Francis Thompson

En este momento, tengo treinta y tres años encima de la
    mesa del despacho
y un pequeño residuo de meses sobre el cenicero de plata.
He preguntado a mis hermanas si saben quién es este hombre
que viene, entre mi hombro y mi hombro, adonde yo vengo,
y vuelve
el rostro si yo lo torno . . .

Siento frío, y no sé qué ponerme por dentro
de la muerte, qué trozo de tierra es el mío,
qué noche es la noche de echarme a morir,
qué látigo verde me heñirá bajo el mar.

A veces me acomete un largo vértigo
y quisiera ser nada más un humoso lego en la orden antigua
    de los muertos,
servirles el silencio con mis propias manos
y meditar en un rincón del claustro de las sombras . . .

Del claustro de las sombras, allí
donde los sueños exaltan sus luces cándidas o pálidas.

THE CLOISTER OF THE SHADES

. . . to the antique order of the dead
—Francis Thompson

At the moment, I have thirty-three years on top of the table
    in my workroom
and a few months left over in the silver ashtray.
I've asked my sisters if they know this man
who comes, between my shoulders, wherever I come
and turns
his face if I turn mine . . .

I feel cold, and I don't know what to put on
under my death, what plot of land is mine,
what night's the night I must make ready for death,
what green whip will knead me under the sea.

Sometimes I am seized by a long vertigo
and I'd like to be nothing but a smoky layman in the antique
    order of the dead,
to serve them silence, to serve it around with my own hands
and meditate in a corner of the cloister of the shades . . .

Of the cloister of the shades, there
where dreams uplift their candid, pale lights.

NI ÉL NI TÚ

A martillazos de cristal, el pecho
espera que el dolor le alumbre un llanto
de música esperanza. Y mientras tanto,
silbo en silencio, contemplando el techo.

Sábanas son el mar, navío el lecho,
sedas hinchadas a favor de espanto,
y para qué cambiar: si me levanto
surco la misma sed que si me echo.

Silba en silencio. Sin salir de casa,
silba a los cuatro vientos del olvido,
a ver si vuelve Dios. A ver qué pasa.

Qué va a pasar. Silencio a martillazos.
Un navío en el mar, y otro perdido
que iba y venía al puerto de mis brazos.

NEITHER HE NOR YOU

Its hammer beating on glass, my heart
waits for anguish to throw light on a weeping
of hopeful music. And during all this,
I whistle silently, looking at the ceiling.

The sheets are the ocean, the bed is a ship,
sails swelled out with fear,
and why should I change: if I get up
I'll plow the same thirst I plow lying down.

Whistle silently. Without leaving the house,
whistle up the four winds of forgetfulness,
to see if God comes back. To see what's happening.

What's going to happen. Hammerstrokes of silence.
One ship at sea, and another lost
that used to come and go in the harbor of my arms.

LO FEO

Nada hay más antiestético que dos sapos desnudos
ni nada más valiente ni libre que los días
el pie de los toreros los pesados escudos
y el cumplimiento exacto de algunas profecías

Nada hay más horroroso que amarse por debajo
ni nada más completo que un surtidor caliente
un ángel que se aplica silencioso al trabajo
y un fabuloso cine lleno de amor y gente

Nada hay más detestable que el té de los amigos
ni nada más dichoso señores que las hojas
el aire que las briza los soñolientos trigos
y acaso acaso las amapolas rojas

Nada hay tan vergonzante tan lleno de tristeza
como un jardín cerrado después de los ponientes
en cada puerta un hombre cuando el amor empieza
a hacer precisas ciertas medidas deprimentes

En cambio las estrellas son blancas como un libro
y fuertes los muchachos que van a los talleres
málaga bella málaga y sin embargo libro
una batalla pálida de sueños y mujeres

El sol el as de oros lo feo me horroriza
como si fuese un ángel de pantalones cortos
desnudas las muñecas y los ojos de tiza
extrayendo raíces de todos los abortos

UGLY THINGS

There's nothing more antiesthetic than two naked toads
nor anything more brave or free than the days
a bullfighter's foot his heavy shield
and the precise fulfillment of certain prophecies

There's nothing more horrifying than to love each other
  underneath
nor anything more complete than a hot-running spout
an angel that quietly devotes himself to his work
and a fabulous movie theater full of love and people

There's nothing more despicable than tea given by friends
nor anything luckier gentlemen than leaves
the air that cradles them the half-asleep wheats
and perhaps perhaps the red poppies

There's nothing so shameful so full of sadness
as a garden locked after sundown
a man in every doorway when love begins
to make certain depressing measures necessary

On the other hand the stars are white as a book
and the boys who go down to the workshops strong
malaga beautiful *malaga* and nevertheless I join
a pale free-for-all of dreams and women

The sun the ace of gold ugliness horrifies me
as if I were an angel in knee pants
wrists naked and eyes like chalk
extracting roots from all the abortions

QUE CADA UNO APORTE LO QUE SEPA

Acontece querer a una persona,
a un sapito, por favor, no lo piséis,
también a un continente como Europa,
continuamente
hendido, herido a quemarropa,
y, simultáneamente, a voz en grito,
otras palabras nos estorban,
tales como "armisticio," "teatro,"
"suspensión de hostilidades," "todo era una broma,"
    y otras.

Pero la gente
lo cree así, y cuelga colgaduras
y echa por la ventana banderas y una alfombra,
como si fuera verdad,
como (se suele decir) si tal cosa . . .

Ocurre, lo he visto con mis propios medios.
Durante veinte años la brisa iba viento en popa,
y se volvieron a ver sombreros de primavera
y parecía que iba a volar la rosa.

En 1939 llamaron a misa a los pobres hombres.
Se desinflaron unas cuantas bombas
y por la noche hubo fuegos japoneses en la bahía.
Estábamos—otra vez—en otra.

Después oí hablar en la habitación de al lado.
(Una mujer desgañitada, loca.)
Lo demás, lo aprendisteis directamente.
Sabíamos de sobra.

LET EACH CONTRIBUTE WHAT HE KNOWS

It so happens that you can love a person,
a little toad, oh please don't step on it,
also a continent like Europe,
continually
split, wounded at close range,
and, simultaneously, pealed out,
other words upset us,
such as "armistice," "theater,"
"suspension of hostilities," "it was all a joke,"
    and others.

But people
believe it's like that, they hang out buntings
and slide banners and tapestries out the window,
as if it were really true,
as if (they're in the habit of saying) such a thing . . .

It happens, I've seen it with my own means.
The breeze coasted along for twenty years
and spring hats were seen about, once more,
and it looked like the rose would fly.

In 1939 they called the poor men out to Mass.
The fuse was pulled out of a few live bombs
and at night there were Japanese fireworks along
    the bay.
We were in the middle of another, once more . . .

Afterwards, I heard voices in the next room.
(A screaming woman, gone out of her mind.)
The rest you yourself learned directly.
We knew more than enough.

PLAÑID ASÍ

Están multiplicando las niñas en alta voz,
yo por ti, tú por mí, los dos
por los que ya no pueden ni con el alma,
cantan las niñas en alta voz
a ver si consiguen que de una vez las oiga Dios.

Yo por ti, tú por mí, todos
por una tierra en paz y una patria mejor.
Las niñas de las escuelas públicas ponen el grito en
    el cielo,
pero parece que el cielo no quiere nada con los
    pobres,
no lo puedo creer. Debe de haber algún error
en el multiplicando o en el multiplicador.

Las que tengan trenzas, que se las suelten,
las que traigan braguitas, que se las bajen rápida-
    mente,
y las que no tengan otra cosa que un pequeño caracol,
que lo saquen al sol,
y todas a la vez entonen en alta voz
yo por ti, tú por mí, los dos
por todos los que sufren en la tierra sin que les
    haga caso Dios.

LAMENT

The little girls are multiplying out loud,
me for you, you for me, and both of us
for those whose soul, even, is really too much
for them, the little girls sing it out loud
to see if they can catch God's ear once and for all.

Me for you, you for me, and all
for a land at peace and a better country.
The public school girls cry out to heaven
but heaven will have nothing to do with the poor,
    it seems;
I can't believe it. There must be some error
in the multiplicand or in the multiplier.

Let those who have braids undo them,
those wearing little underpants drop them
quickly and those with nothing but a tiny seashell
put it out in the sun,
and let all of them recite out loud
me for you, you for me, and both of us
for all who suffer on this earth without so much as
    a peep from God.

PASO A PASO

Tachia, los hombres sufren. No tenemos
ni un pedazo de paz con que aplacarles;
roto casi el navío y ya sin remos . . .
¿Qué podemos hacer, qué luz alzarles?

Larga es la noche, Tachia. Oscura y larga
como mis brazos hacia el cielo. Lenta
como la luna desde el mar. Amarga
como el amor: yo llevo bien la cuenta.

Tiempo de soledad es éste. Suena
en Europa el tambor de proa a popa.
Ponte la muerte por los hombros. Ven. A-
lejémonos de Europa.

Pobre, mi pobre Tachia. No tenemos
una brizna de luz para los hombres.
Brama el odio, van rotos rumbo y remos . . .
No quedan de los muertos ni los nombres.

Oh, no olvidamos, no podrá el olvido
vencer sus ojos contra el cielo abiertos.
Larga es la noche, Tachia.
                    . . . Escucha el ruido
del alba abriéndose paso—a paso—entre los muertos.

STEP BY STEP

Tachia, men suffer. We haven't even
a scrap of peace with which to ease them;
the ship almost a wreck, without oars . . .
What can we do, what light hold up for them?

The night is long, Tachia. Dark and long
as my heavenward arms. Slow
as the moon at sea. Bitter
as love: I've kept the figures carefully.

This is the time for loneliness. The drum
rolls from the prow of Europe to its stern.
Put death behind you. Come.
Let's pull away from Europe.

Poor Tachia, my poor thing. We haven't even
a speck of light for man.
Hate bellows. Broken our course and our oars . . .
Of the dead, not even their names are left.

Oh, we haven't forgotten, forgetfulness can't
defeat their eyes, open in the face of heaven.
The night is long, Tachia.
                    . . . Listen to the sound
        of daybreak
opening its way step—by step—between the dead.

MUNDO

Cuando San Agustín escribía sus *Soliloquios*.
Cuando el último soldado alemán se desmoronaba de asco y
   de impotencia.
Cuando las guerras púnicas
y las mujeres abofeteadas en el descansillo de una escalera,
entonces,

cuando San Agustín escribía *La ciudad de Dios* con una mano
y con la otra tomaba notas a fin de combatir las herejías,
precisamente entonces,
cuando ser prisionero de guerra no significaba la muerte, sino
   la casualidad de encontrarse vivo,
cuando las pérfidas mujeres inviolables se dedicaban a re-
   parar las constelaciones deterioradas,
y los encendedores automáticos desfallecían de póstuma
   ternura,

entonces, ya lo he dicho,
San Agustín andaba corrigiendo las pruebas de su *Enchiridion
   ad Laurentium*
y los soldados alemanes se orinaban encima de los niños
   recién bombardeados.

Triste, triste es el mundo,
como una muchacha huérfana de padre a quien los salte-
   adores de abrazos sujetan contra un muro.
Muchas veces hemos pretendido que la soledad de los hom-
   bres se llenase de lágrimas.
Muchas veces, infinitas veces hemos dejado de dar la mano

WORLD

When St. Augustine was writing his *Soliloquies*.
When the last German soldier was going to pieces from loath-
  ing and impotence.
At the time of the Punic wars
and the women slapped about on stairway landings,
then,

when St. Augustine was writing *The City of God* with one
  hand
and with the other took notes for his campaign against the
  heresies,
precisely then,
when being a prisoner of war did not mean death, but only
  that one still happened to be alive,
when the faithless inviolable women spent time repairing the
  damaged constellations,
and the cigarette lighters failed miserably from a feeling of
  posthumous tenderness,

then, I've already mentioned it,
St. Augustine was in the process of correcting the proofs for
  his *Enchiridion ad Laurentium*
and the German soldiers were urinating on the recently
  bombed children.

Sad, sad is the world,
like a fatherless girl whom the robbers of embraces pin
  against a wall.
We have hoped, a great number of times, men's solitude
  would fill with tears.

y no hemos conseguido otra cosa que unas cuantas arenillas
  pertinazmente intercaladas entre los dientes.

Oh si San Agustín se hubiese enterado de que la diplomacia
  europea
andaba comprometida con artistas de *variétés* de muy
  dudosa reputación,
y que el ejército norteamericano acostumbraba recibir
  paquetes donde la más ligera falta de ortografía
era aclamada como venturoso presagio de la libertad de los
  pueblos oprimidos por el endoluminismo.

Voy a llorar de tanta pierna rota
y de tanto cansancio que se advierte en los poetas menores
  de dieciocho años.

Nunca se ha conocido un desastre igual.
Hasta las Hermanas de la Caridad hablan de crisis
y se escriben gruesos volúmenes sobre la decadencia del
  jabón de afeitar entre los esquimales.

Decid adónde vamos a parar con tanta angustia
y tanto dolor de padres desconocidos entre sí.

Cuando San Agustín se entere de que los teléfonos auto-
  máticos han dejado de funcionar
y de que las tarifas contra incendios se han ocultado tími-
  damente en la cabellera de las muchachitas rubias,
ah entonces, cuando San Agustín lo sepa todo
un gran rayo descenderá sobre la tierra y en un abrir y cerrar
  de ojos nos volveremos todos idiotas.

A great, an infinite number of times, we have refused to
    shake hands
and gained nothing but a few grains of saltpeter stubbornly
    worked in between our teeth.

Oh if St. Augustine had discovered that European diplomats
were tied up with stage people of very questionable reputa-
    tions
and that the American army used to receive packages on
    which the slightest spelling error
was acclaimed as a lucky sign of the imminent liberation of
    the peoples oppressed by endoluminism.

I am going to cry over so many smashed human limbs
and so much fatigue plain in poets under eighteen.

Never has such a disaster been known.
Even the Sisters of Charity talk of a crisis
and fat volumes are written on the decline in the quality of
    shaving soap among the Eskimos.

Tell me, just where can we end up, with so much anguish
and so much grief in parents who don't even know one
    another.

When St. Augustine learns that the public telephones are out
    of order
and that the fire insurance premiums have been shyly hidden
    in the hair of little blond girls,
ah then, when St. Augustine knows everything,
a big bolt of lightning will descend on earth and in a wink
    we're all going to turn into raving idiots.

187

HIJOS DE LA TIERRA

Parece como si el mundo caminase de espaldas
hacia la noche enorme de los acantilados.
Que un hombre, a hombros del miedo, trepase por las faldas
hirsutas de la muerte, con los ojos cerrados.

Europa, amontonada sobre España, en escombros;
sin norte, Norteamérica, cayéndose hacia arriba;
recién nacida, Rusia, sangrándole los hombros;
Oriente, dando tumbos; y el resto, a la deriva.

Parece como si el mundo me mirase a los ojos,
que quisiera decirme no sé qué, de rodillas;
alza al cielo las manos, me da a oler sus manojos
de muertos, entre gritos y un trepidar de astillas.

El mar, puesto de pie,
le pega en la garganta con un látigo verde;
le descantilla; de
repente, echando espuma por la boca, le muerde.

Parece como si el mundo se acabase, se hundiera.
Parece como si Dios, con los ojos abiertos,
a los hijos del hombre los ojos les comiera.
(No le bastan—parece—los ojos de los muertos.)

Europa, a hombros de España, hambrienta y sola;
los Estados de América, saliéndose de madre;
la bandera de Rusia, oh sedal de ola en ola;
Asia, la inmensa flecha que el futuro taladre.

¡Alzad al cielo el vientre, oh hijos de la tierra;
salid por esas calles dando gritos de espanto!
Los veintitrés millones de muertos en la guerra
se agolpan ante un cielo cerrado a cal y canto.

CHILDREN OF THE PLANET

It's as if the world were taking great steps backward
toward the giant night of the cliffs.
And a man, on the shoulders of fear, were climbing
the stiff-haired foothills of death, with his eyes closed.

Europe, piled on top of Spain, in ruins;
North America, off course, falling upwards;
infant Russia, bleeding from its shoulders;
the East, staggering; and the rest, drifting.

It's as if the world were looking into my eyes,
wanting to tell me something, on its knees;
it lifts its hands to heaven, it gives me sheaves
of corpses to smell, among screams and quivering splinters.

The sea, now standing up,
strikes the throat of the world with a green whip;
splits it open; then
suddenly, froth leaping from its mouth, sinks its teeth in.

It's as if the world were ending, going under.
It's as if God, with his eyes open,
were feeding on the eyes of the children of men.
(Evidently the eyes of the dead are not enough.)

Europe, on Spain's shoulders, full of hunger, alone;
the United States of America, spilling over;
the Russian flag, oh line cast into wave after wave;
Asia, the immense arrow drilling into the future.

Lift your belly to the sky, oh children of the planet!
Run into the streets screaming with terror!
The twenty-three million corpses of this war
crowd before a heaven walled up with plaster and lime.

Pido la paz y la palabra
(I Ask for Peace and the
Right to Speak, 1955)

A LA INMENSA MAYORÍA

Aquí tenéis, en canto y alma, al hombre
aquel que amó, vivió, murió por dentro
y un buen día bajó a la calle: entonces
comprendió: y rompió todos sus versos.

Así es, así fué. Salió una noche
echando espuma por los ojos, ebrio
de amor, huyendo sin saber adónde:
adonde el aire no apestase a muerto.

Tiendas de paz, brizados pabellones,
eran sus brazos, como llama al viento;
olas de sangre contra el pecho, enormes
olas de odio, ved, por todo el cuerpo.

¡Aquí! ¡Llegad! ¡Ay! Angeles atroces
en vuelo horizontal cruzan el cielo;
horribles peces de metal recorren
las espaldas del mar, de puerto a puerto.

Yo doy todos mis versos por un hombre
en paz. Aquí tenéis, en carne y hueso,
mi última voluntad. Bilbao, a once
de abril, cincuenta y tantos.

Blas de Otero.

TO THE IMMENSE MAJORITY

Here, in poetry and soul, you have a man
who loved, lived, died on the inside
and one day went outside: then
he understood, and tore up all his poems.

It's true, that's how it was. He went out one night,
foam leaping from his eyes, drunk
with love, running he didn't know where:
where the air was not full of the stink of corpses.

His arms were peace tents,
flapping canopies, like flames in the wind;
waves of blood against his chest, huge
waves of hatred, all through his body.

This way! Come! Oh, hideous angels
fly parallel with the earth across the sky;
hideous fish made of steel cross
the shoulders of the ocean from port to port.

I would give all of my poems for a man
at peace. Here, in flesh and blood,
you have my final will. Bilbao, April
eleventh, during the fifties.

Blas de Otero.

EN EL PRINCIPIO

Si he perdido la vida, el tiempo, todo
lo que tiré, como un anillo, al agua,
si he perdido la voz en la maleza,
me queda la palabra.

Si he sufrido la sed, el hambre, todo
lo que era mío y resultó ser nada,
si he segado las sombras en silencio,
me queda la palabra.

Si abrí los labios para ver el rostro
puro y terrible de mi patria,
si abrí los labios hasta desgarrármelos,
me queda la palabra.

IN THE BEGINNING

If I have lost life, time, everything
I threw, like a ring, into the water,
if I have lost my voice among the weeds,
I still have words.

If I have suffered thirst, hunger, everything
I owned and turned out to be nothing,
if I have harvested the shadows silently,
I still have words.

If I opened my lips to look into the clear
terrible face of my country, if I opened
my lips until they came off in shreds,
I still have words.

GALLARTA

*(el hierro es vizcaíno, que os encargo,
corto en palabras, pero en obras largo.
—Tirso de Molina)*

Acaso el mar. Tampoco. El hombre acaso.
Es el otoño. Hermoso dios. La tierra
roja. La piedra, roja. Acaso, un árbol
como la sangre. Hermoso dios. La piedra
y el hombre.

Es el otoño. Entonces. Caminábamos
hacia la cima. El mar en letra impresa.
Corto en palabras, pero en olas ancho.
Hacia las cinco de la tarde. Ortuella
y el aire.

Entonces. Entornó, no sé, los párpados
ella. Hermoso dios de la miseria.
Y, ya en la llambria, a vista de barranco,
el hierro.

Rey de los ojos. Sófocles roñado.
Hundida silla sideral. Paciencia.
Vizcaíno es el hierro—el mar, cantábrico—,
corto en palabras. Ley de los poemas
míos.

GALLARTA

(the iron I warn you about is from Biscaya, short,
when it comes to words, but in action long.
                                —Tirso de Molina)*

The sea perhaps. Not that, either. Perhaps
man. It is autumn. Handsome god. The earth,
red. Red the stone. Perhaps a tree
like blood. Handsome god. The stone
and man.

It's autumn. Then. And we were walking
to the top. The sea, printed in letters.
Short, when it comes to words, but long in waves.
Towards five in the afternoon. Ortuella
and the air.

Then. She dropped her eyelids, I don't know—
halfway. Handsome god of misery.
And, on the rock's steep face now, seen from the cliff,
the iron.

King of eyes. Tarnished Sophocles.
Sunken chair of stars. Patience.
The iron is Biscayan—the sea, Cantabrian—
short, when it comes to words. The law my poems
follow.

BIOTZ–BEGIETAN

Ahora
voy a contar la historia de mi vida
en un abecedario ceniciento.
El país de los ricos rodeando mi cintura

y todo lo demás. Escribo y callo.
Yo nací de repente, no recuerdo
si era sol o era lluvia o era jueves.
Manos de lana me enredaran, madre.

Madeja arrebatada de tus brazos
blancos, hoy me contemplo como un ciego,
oigo tus pasos en la niebla, vienen
a enhebrarme la vida destrozada.

Aquellos hombres me abrasaron, hablo
del hielo aquel de luto atormentado,
la derrota del niño y su caligrafía
triste, trémula flor desfigurada.

Madre, no me mandes más a coger miedo
y frío ante un pupitre con estampas.
Tú enciendes la verdad como una lágrima,
dame la mano, guárdame
en tu armario de luna y de manteles.

Esto es Madrid, me han dicho unas mujeres
arrodilladas en sus delantales,
este es el sitio
donde enterraron un gran ramo verde
y donde está mi sangre reclinada.

BIOTZ–BEGIETAN

Now
I am going to tell the story of my life
in an alphabet of ashes.
The land of the rich looped round my waist

and all the rest. I write and don't speak out.
I was born suddenly, I don't remember
if it was sunny or rainy or Thursday.
Hands of wool entangled me, mother.

Skein torn out of your white arms,
I examine myself today like a blind man,
I hear your footsteps in the fog
coming to string my broken life.

Certain men set me on fire once, I speak
of a tormented mourning cold like ice,
the child's defeat and his pitiful
script, tremulous disfigured flower.

Mother, don't send me out to catch fear
and cold at a school desk full of holy pictures.
You light truth like a tear,
give me your hand, and keep me safe
in the closet with the moonlight and the linens.

This is Madrid, I was told
by some women kneeling on their aprons,
this is the spot
where they buried a huge green branch
on which my blood is leaning.

Días de hambre, escándalos de hambre,
misteriosas sandalias
aliándose a las sombras del romero
y el laurel asesino. Escribo y callo.

Aquí junté la letra a la palabra,
la palabra al papel.
                    Y esto es París,
me dijeron los ángeles, la gente
lo repetía, esto es París. *Peut être*,
allí sufrí las iras del espíritu

y tomé ejemplo de la torre Eiffel.

Esta es la historia de mi vida,
dije, y tampoco era. Escribo y callo.

Days of hunger, scandals about hunger,
mysterious sandals
sidling up to the shadows of the rosemary
and the murderous laurel. I write and don't speak out.

This is where I joined each letter to its word
and each word to its paper.
                                And this is Paris,
the angels said to me, and people repeated it,
this is Paris. *Peut être,*
that's where I suffered the angers of the spirit

and followed in the Eiffel Tower's steps.

This is the story of my life, I said,
and it really wasn't. I write and I don't speak out.

JUICIO FINAL

Yo, pecador, artista del pecado,
comido por el ansia hasta los tuétanos,
yo, tropel de esperanza y de fracasos,
estatua del dolor, firma del viento.

Yo, pecador, en fin, desesperado
de sombras y de sueños: me confieso
que soy un hombre en situación de hablaros
de la vida. Pequé. No me arrepiento.

Nací para narrar con estos labios
que barrerá la muerte un día de éstos,
espléndidas caídas en picado
del bello avión aquel de carne y hueso.

Alas arriba disparó los brazos,
alardeando de tan alto invento;
plumas de níquel: escribid despacio.
Helas aquí, hincadas en el suelo.

Este es mi sitio. Mi terreno. Campo
de aterrizaje de mis ansias. Cielo
al revés. Es mi sitio y no lo cambio
por ninguno. Caí. No me arrepiento.

Ímpetus nuevos nacerán, más altos.
Llegaré por mis pies—¿para qué os quiero?—
a la patria del hombre: al cielo raso
de sombras ésas y de sueños ésos.

LAST JUDGMENT

I, sinner, poet of sin,
whom anxiety has eaten away to the bone,
I, a tangle of hope and disasters,
statue of suffering, signature of the wind.

I, sinner, in fact, driven to the wall
by shadows and dreams, confess I'm a man
in a position to talk to you
about life. I've sinned. And I'm not sorry.

I was born to describe with these lips
death will sweep away one of these days
how this fine aircraft of flesh and bone
went into marvelous nosedives.

He let his arms fly out like wings,
making too much of this high invention;
the feathers were nickel: write slowly.
Here they are, driven into the ground.

This is my place. My territory. Landing
strip of my anxieties. Heaven
upside down. It's my place, and I won't change it
for another. I fell, and I'm not sorry.

New flights will be born, even higher.
I'll arrive on my feet—why else do I need you?—
in the country of man: in the open sky
full of those shadows and those dreams.

UN VASO EN LA BRISA

Calvario como el mío pocos he visto. Ven,
asómate a esta ventana.
Para qué voy a escribir lo que ha ocurrido.
El tiempo todo lo aclara.

Para qué hablar de este hombre cuando hay tantos
　　que esperan
(españahogándose) un poco de luz, nada
más, un vaso de luz
que apague la sed de sus almas.

Lo mejor será que me someta a la tempestad,
todo tiene su término, mañana
por la mañana hará sol
y podré salir al campo. Mientras el río pasa.

No esperéis que me dé por vencido.
Es mucho lo que tengo apostado a esa carta.
Malditos sean los que se ensañaron
en mi silencio con sus palabras.

Yo ofrezco mi vida a los dioses
que habitan el país de la esperanza
y me inclino a la tierra y acepto
la brisa que agita levemente esta página . . .

A GLASS IN THE BREEZE

I've seen few Calvaries like the one I have. Come,
come over to this window.
Why should I write down what's happened.
Time will make it all clear.

Why talk of this man when there are so many others waiting
(smothering in Spain) for a bit of light, that's
all, just a glassful of light
to stop the thirst in their souls.

I may as well bow before the storm,
everything has an end, tomorrow
morning, it will be sunny,
and I can go to the country. Meanwhile, the river goes by.

Don't expect me to take it lying down.
I've staked everything on this one card.
God damn those on top who sniped
at my silence with their words.

I offer my life to the gods
who live in the country of hope
and I bend down to the earth and accept
the breeze that gently troubles this page . . .

"ME LLAMARÁN"

*. . . porque la mayor locura que puede hacer un hombre
en esta vida es dejarse morir, sin más ni más . . .*

Sancho.
(*Quixote*, II, cap. 74.)

1

Me llamarán, nos llamarán a todos.
Tú, y tú, y yo, nos turnaremos,
en tornos de cristal, ante la muerte.
Y te expondrán, nos expondremos todos
a ser trizados ¡zas! por una bala.

Bien lo sabéis. Vendrán
por ti, por ti, por mí, por todos.
Y también
por ti.
(Aquí
no se salva ni dios. Lo asesinaron.)

Escrito está. Tu nombre está ya listo,
temblando en un papel. Aquél que dice:
abel, abel, abel . . . o *yo, tú, él . . .*

2

Pero tú, Sancho Pueblo,
pronuncias anchas sílabas,
permanentes palabras que no lleva el viento . . .

"THEY WILL CALL ME"

*. . . for the biggest madness a man can be guilty of in
this life is to let himself die, just like that . . .*

Sancho.
(*Quixote*, II, chap. 74.)

1

They will call me, they will call us all.
You, and you, and I will take our turn,
like revolving glass, before death.
And they will expose you, we will all be
exposed to being splintered, zip! by a bullet.

How well you know it. They will come
for you, for you, for me, for all of us.
And also for
you.
(Here
not even god can save his skin. They murdered him.)

It is written. Your name is ready now,
trembling on a sheet of paper. The one that says:
abel, abel, abel . . . or *I, you, he . . .*

2

But you, Sancho People,
pronounce widespread syllables,
permanent words the wind does not carry . . .

VENCER JUNTOS

A las puertas del mundo.

Estoy llamando al día con las manos mojadas,
a las puertas del mundo, mientras crece la sangre.

Yo soy un hombre literalmente amado
por todas las desgracias—y gracias que es tan
    grande la esperanza!
Un español de arriba de los ríos,
Guadalquivir y el Ebro me guardan las espaldas.

A las puertas del mundo estoy llamando,
mientras la sangre avanza.

Subo a la torre, alrededor del día
arden las rosas de los muertos, planto
palmas de menta escandalizadoras.
Dejo la juncia, los geiseres junto,
esgrimo las más verdes esmeraldas.

Doy con los labios en la aurora, llamo
a las puertas del mundo,
salto a las torres de la paz, hermosas,
mezo otras brisas, otros temas rozo.

Oh patria, árbol de sangre, lóbrega
España.

Abramos juntos
el último capullo del futuro.

WE SHALL OVERCOME

At the doors of the world.

I call out to the day with wet hands,
at the doors of the world, while the blood grows.

I am a man literally loved by all sorts
of ruin—and there's lots of hope too, thank God.
A Spaniard from beyond the rivers,
Guadalquivir and Ebro guard my back.

I am calling at the doors of the world,
while blood advances.

I ascend the tower, the roses of the dead
are burning around the day, I plant
outrageous sprigs of mint.
I leave the sedge, fasten geysers together,
and flash the greenest emeralds.

I knock on the dawn with my lips,
I call at the doors of the world,
I leap up to the beautiful towers of peace,
I sway other breezes and touch other themes.

O my country, tree of blood, darkling
Spain.

*Let us open together
the last bud of the future.*

FIDELIDAD

Creo en el hombre. He visto
espaldas astilladas a trallazos,
almas cegadas avanzando a brincos
(españas a caballo
del dolor y del hambre). Y he creído.

Creo en la paz. He visto
altas estrellas, llameantes ámbitos
amanecientes, incendiando ríos
hondos, caudal humano
hacia otra luz: he visto y he creído.

Creo en ti, patria. Digo
lo que he visto: relámpagos
de rabia, amor en frío, y un cuchillo
chillando, haciéndose pedazos
de pan: aunque hoy hay sólo sombra, he visto
y he creído.

FIDELITY

I have faith in man. I have seen
backs split open by the lash,
blinded souls jerking forward
(Spains mounted
on hunger and pain). And I've kept faith.

I have faith in peace. I have seen
tall stars, boundaries of dawn
bursting into flame, setting deep
rivers on fire, a human stream
toward some other light: I saw and I've kept faith.

I have faith in you, my country. I tell
what I have seen: thunderbolts
of anger, love in cold blood, and a knife
screaming, carving itself into pieces
of bread: everything looks dark now, but I saw
and I kept faith.

from

En castellano
(In Plain Words, 1959)

COPLA DEL RÍO

Recuerde el alma dormida
el río que con paso casi humano,
enfurecido de aridarse en vano,
desembocó en la vida.

Esta es, así era el sitio, el agua
que ni varió de limpia ni de río,
hoy como ayer, ayer como fontana,
y hoy como nunca de galán crecido.

Y pues vos, claro varón, tanta esperanza
y aún más, y mayor fe que don Rodrigo
Manrique hoy acodáis hacia el mañana,
andad en paz
                        apacentando el trigo . . .

SONG OF THE RIVER

Let the sleeping soul remember
the river that with an almost human
step, angry at running dry
in vain, stumbled out into life.

This, the place was just like this, is the water
that never left off being clear or river,
today like yesterday, yesterday only a spring,
and today grown a greater figure than ever.

And now, gallant sir, thou leanest out so much
hope, even more, and greater faith, than
Don Rodrigo Manrique towards tomorrow, go
in peace
        herding the wheat out to pasture . . .

MUY LEJOS

Unas mujeres, tristes y pintadas,
sonreían a todas las carteras,
y ellos, analfabetos y magnánimos,
las miraban por dentro, hacia las medias.

Oh cuánta sed, cuánto mendigo en faldas
de eternidad. Ciudad llena de iglesias
y casas públicas, donde el hombre es harto
y el hambre se reparte a manos llenas.

Bendecida ciudad llena de manchas,
plagada de adulterios e indulgencias;
ciudad donde las almas son de barro
y el barro embarra todas las estrellas.

Laboriosa ciudad, salmo de fábricas
donde el hombre maldice, mientras rezan
los presidentes de Consejo: oh altos
hornos, infiernos hondos en la niebla.

Las tres y cinco de la madrugada.
Puertas, puertas y puertas. Y más puertas.
Junto al Nervión un hombre está meando.
Pasan dos guardias en sus bicicletas.

Y voy mirando escaparates. *Paca
y Luz. Hijos de tal.* Medias de seda.
Devocionarios. Más devocionarios.
Libros de misa. Tules. Velos. Velas.

FAR AWAY

A few women, sad and rouged,
used to smile at all the wallets
and in turn they, illiterate but generous,
looked inside *them*, up along their stockings.

Oh how much thirst, how many beggars in skirts
of eternity. City filled with churches
and public houses, where man stuffs himself
and hunger is passed out by the handful.

Blessed city covered with stains,
infested with adulteries and indulgences,
city where souls are made of clay
and clay muddies all the stars.

Industrious city, psalm of factories
where man says his *damns*, while the Chairmen
of the Board say their prayers: blast
furnaces, oh deep hells in the mist.

3:05 A.M.
Doors, doors and doors. And more doors.
A man takes a piss down by the Nervion.
Two cops go by on bicycles.

And I walk along looking in shop windows.
"Paca & Luz." "Sons of such & such." Silk
stockings. Prayer books. And more prayer books.
Missals. Tulles. Veils. Candles.

Y novenitas de la Inmaculada.
Arriba, es el jolgorio de las piernas
trenzadas. Oh ese barrio del escándalo . . .
Pero duermen tranquilas las doncellas.

Y voy silbando por la calle. Nada
me importas tú, ciudad donde naciera.
Ciudad donde, muy lejos, muy lejano,
se escucha el mar, la mar de Dios, inmensa.

And novenas to the Immaculate Conception.
Upstairs, a bang-up time of interlocked
legs. Oh that neighborhood of scandalous doings . . .
But nice girls sleep on peacefully.

And I go whistling down the street. You mean
nothing to me, city where I was born.
City where far away, a very long way off,
the sea can be heard, the immense sea of God.

PALABRAS REUNIDAS PARA
ANTONIO MACHADO

Un corazón solitario
no es un corazón.

A.M.

Si me atreviera
a hablarte, a responderte,
pero no soy,
solo,
nadie.

Entonces,
cierro las manos, llamo a tus raíces,
estoy
oyendo el lento ayer:
el romancero
y el cancionero popular; el recio
són de Jorge Manrique;
la palabra cabal
de fray Luis; el chasquido
de Quevedo;
de pronto,
toco la tierra que borró tus brazos,
el mar
donde amarró la nave que pronto ha de volver.

Ahora,
removidos los surcos (el primero
es llamado Gonzalo de Berceo),
pronuncio
unas pocas palabras verdaderas.

WORDS PUT TOGETHER FOR
ANTONIO MACHADO

A heart by itself
is not a heart.
> A.M.

If I could draw up the courage
to speak to, and answer, you,
but, by myself,
I am
no one.

Well,
I close my hands, call out your roots,
I am
listening to a slow yesterday:
to the *Romancero*
and the popular *Cancionero*; the rough
meters of Jorge Manrique;
the exact word
of Fray Luis; Quevedo's
whiplash;
suddenly
I feel out the earth that has erased your arms,
the sea
where the ship tied up, that shortly must return.

Now
that the furrows have been turned up (the first
one's name is Gonzalo de Berceo),
I'll say
a few words that are true.

Áquellas
con que pedí la paz y la palabra:

Árboles abolidos,
volveréis a brillar
al sol. Olmos sonoros, altos
álamos, lentas encinas,
olivo
en paz,
árboles de una patria árida y triste,
entrad
a pie desnudo en el arroyo claro,
fuente serena de la libertad.

Silencio.

Sevilla está llorando. Soria
se puso seria. Baeza
alza al cielo las hoces (los olivos
recuerdan una brisa granadamente triste).
El mar
se derrama hacia Francia, te reclama,
quiere, queremos
tenerte, convivirte,
                compartirte
como el pan.

Those
with which I asked for peace and the right to speak:

> *Outlawed trees,*
> *you will shine again*
> *in the sun. Musical elms, tall*
> *poplars, sluggish oaks,*
> *olive tree*
> *at peace,*
> *trees of a barren and sad land,*
> *enter*
> *the clear stream in your bare feet,*
> *peaceful waters of freedom.*

Silence.

Seville is crying. Soria
has turned serious. Baeza
lifts sickles to the sky (the olive trees
recall a sad breeze ready to be reaped).
The sea
falls headlong towards France, claims
you, it wants, we want
to have you, to have you live with us,
                              to share you

like bread.

CARTAS Y POEMAS A NAZIM HIKMET
(1958– . . .)

Puesto que tú me has conmovido,
en este tiempo en que es tan difícil la ternura,
y tu palabra se abre como la puerta de tu celda
frente al Mármara,
rasgo el papel y, de hermano a hermano, hablo contigo
(*acaban de sonar
               las nueve de la noche*)
de cosas que no existen: Dios
está escuchando detrás de la puerta
de tu celda, cedida por amor al hombre:

                             Nazim Hikmet,
quédate con nosotros.

Que tu palabra entre entre las rejas de esta vieja cárcel
alzada sobre el Cantábrico,
que golpee en España
como una espada en el campo de Dumlupinar,
que los ríos la rueden hacia Levante y por Andalucía se
    extienda
como un mantel de tela pobre y cálida,
sobre la mesa de la miseria madre.

Te ruego te quedes con nosotros,
es todo lo que podemos ofrecerte: diecinueve años
perdidos,
peor que perdidos, gastados,
más que gastados, rotos

LETTERS AND POEMS TO NAZIM HIKMET
(1958– . . .)

Considering how you have moved me
at this time when tenderness is so difficult
and your word opens like the door of your cell
in front of the Marmara,
I scratch paper and, brother to brother, speak with you
(*it has just struck*
$\qquad$ *9:00* P.M.)
about things that don't exist: God
is eavesdropping behind the door
of your cell, awarded for loving your fellowman:
$\hfill$ Nazim Hikmet,
stay with us.

Let your word enter through the bars of this old prison
erect above the Cantabrian,
let it sound out in Spain
like a sword in the field of Dumlupinar,
let rivers roll it towards Levante and let it spread over
$\qquad$ Andalucía
like a tablecloth of cheap but warm material
over mother Misery's table.

I beg you to stay with us,
all we can offer you is nineteen
lost years,
worse than lost, wasted,
more than wasted, broken

dentro del alma:
                    ten
misericordia de mi espúrea España.

Nunca oíste mi nombre ni lo has de oír, acaso,
estamos separados por mares, por montañas, por mi maldito
        encierro,
voluntario a fuerza de amor,
soy sólo poeta, pero en serio,
sufrí como cualquiera, menos
que muchos que no escribén porque no saben, otros
que no hablan porque no pueden, muertos
de miedo o de hambre
(aquí decimos *A falta de pan, buenas son tortas*, se cumplió)

pero habla, escribe tú, Nazim Hikmet,
cuenta por ahí lo que te he dicho, háblanos
del viento del Este y la verdad del día,
aquí entre sombras te suplico, escúchanos.

inside the soul:
                    have
mercy on my distorted Spain.

You've never heard my name and you never will, perhaps,
we are separated by seas, by mountains, by my accursed
     imprisonment,
voluntary, thanks to love,
I'm only a poet, but an honest one,
I suffered like anybody else, less
than many who don't write because they don't know how,
     others
who don't speak because they can't, scared
or starved to death
(here we say *If there is no bread, sticks will do*, it was
     fulfilled)

but speak, write, Nazim Hikmet,
tell over there what I have told you, speak
to us about the East wind and what's true each day,
here, among shadows, I beg you, hear us.

CENSORIA

Se durmió en la cocina como un trapo.
No le alcanzaba el jornal ni para morirse.
Se dejó caer en la banqueta como un trapo
y se escurrió por el sueño, sin olvidar . . .

Usualmente, paren los humildes esas niñas escrofulosas
que portan únicamente una sayita deshilachada sobre los
      huesos.
¡Salid corriendo a verlas, hipócritas!
¡Escribid al cielo lo que aquí pasa!
¡Sobornad a vuestros monitores para admirar esto!
Españolitos helándose
al sol—no exactamente el de justicia.

Voy a protestar, estoy protestando dese hace mucho tiempo;
me duele tanto el dolor, que a veces
pego saltos en mitad de la calle,
y no he de callar por más que con el dedo
me persignen la frente, y los labios, y el verso.

CENSORED

She fell asleep in the kitchen like a dishrag.
Her job didn't earn enough to die on.
She let herself slip onto the kitchen bench like a rag,
and slipped into sleep, without forgetting . . .

The poor as a matter of course give birth to those scrofulous
    girls
who wear nothing but one old worn-out dress over their
    bones.

Run out and look at them, you hypocrites!
Write to heaven about the situation here!
Corrupt your student teachers into gaping at this!
Spanish children freezing
in the sun . . . not exactly the sun of justice.

I'm going to protest, I've been protesting a long time;
their pain makes me suffer so much that sometimes
I jump up and down in the middle of the street,
and I won't shut up, no matter how much they make the
    sign
of the cross on my forehead, or my lips, or my poems.

from

Esto no es un libro

(This Is Not a Book, 1963)

AÑO MUERTO, AÑO NUEVO

Otro año más. España en sombra. Espesa
sombra en los hombros. Luz de hipocresía
en la frente. Luz yerta. Sombra fría.
Tierra agrietada. Mar. Cielo que pesa.

Si esta es mi patria, mi verguenza es esa
desde el Cantábrico hasta Andalucía.
Olas de rabia. Tierra de maría
santísima, miradla: hambrienta y presa.

Entré en mi casa; vi que amancillada
mi propia juventud yacía inerte;
amancillada, pero no vencida.

Inerte, nunca desesperanzada.
Otro año más camino de la muerte,
hasta que nazca España a nueva vida.

DEAD YEAR, NEW YEAR

One more year. Spain in darkness. Thick
darkness on her shoulders. Hypocrisy's light
on her countenance. Hard light. Cold darkness.
Land full of cracks. Sea. Heavy skies.

If this is my country, it's my cross
from the Cantabrian to Andalusia.
Waves of fury. Land of holy mother
of god, look at it: a hungry prisoner.

I went into my house; saw that my own
youth lay without life, its good name smeared;
its good name smeared, but not defeated.

Without life, never without hope.
One more year on the way to death,
until Spain is born once more.

from

Que trata de España

(All about Spain, 1964)

ESCRITO CON LLUVIA

Ahora es cuando puedes empezar a morirte,
distráete un poco después de haber terminado tu séptimo
    libro,
ahora puedes abandonar los brazos a lo largo del tiempo
y aspirar profundamente entornando los párpados,
piensa en nada
y olvida el daño que te hiciste,
la espalda de Matilde
y su sexo convexo,
ahora mira la lluvia esparcida por el mes de noviembre,
las luces de la ciudad
y el dinero que cae en migajas los sábados a las seis,
espera
el despertar temible de iberoamérica
y comienza a peinarte, a salir a la calle, a seguir
laborando por todos
los que callan, y avanzan, y protestan y empuñan
la luz como cuchillo o la paz como un fusil.

WRITTEN IN RAIN

This is the time when you can begin to die,
take things easy after completing your seventh book,
now you can let your arms fall to your sides in the corridor
    of time,
and breathe deeply, pulling your eyelids shut,
think of nothing
and forget the wrong you've done yourself,
Mathilda's back
and the curve of her sex,
look now at the rain scattered among the days of November,
the city lights
and the money that falls in little crumbs on Saturdays at six,
wait
for the terrible awakening of Latin America
and start to comb your hair, to go out, to keep on
working for all those
who say nothing, and keep on walking, and protest, and hold
the light in their fist like a knife or peace like a gun.

Alegría, parece
que vuelves de la fiesta,
con un clavel de fuego
y la mirada alerta,
árboles inclinados
como personas, ciega
capa de torear
color azul y fresa,
alegría, este otoño
has abierto la puerta
de hierros herrumbrosos,
saltó a la carretera
un perro rojo, el mar
crujió como una seda,
a lo lejos, los montes
de León espejean
tal una espada azul
movida entre la niebla,
alegría,
　　　　paciencia
de la patria que sufre
y la españa que espera.

WAVED IN THE MIST

Gaiety, it seems
you're back from the party
with a carnation of fire
and your eyes wide open,
trees craning
as if they were persons, blind
bullfighter's cape
blue and strawberry
colored, gaiety, this fall
you opened the gate
with its rusty irons,
a red dog dashed out
into the highway, the sea
rustled like silk,
far off, the mountains
of León glitter
like a blue sword
waved in the mist,
gaiety,
      patience
of the land that suffers
and the Spain that waits.

Sentado está, sentado
sobre su propia sombra corrosiva,
a la derecha, dios, y a la izquierda, inclinado,
el hijo. Y el espíritu santo en el aire, a la deriva.
¿Quién ha puesto esta cara
cadavérica? ¿Quién comió de su hambre y ha brindado
con su sed? Ni dios le ampara.
He aquí a su hijo: sordomudo,
y a Teresa, la hija, en una casa de salud o
más crudamente, manicomio.
                                        ¡Mina
de los demonios! ¡Paraíso
subterrenal de tal o cual patrono!

Su compañera, de moza, dicen que era divina.
Ahora es como un paraguas roto. No
quiere ni oir hablar del paraíso.
Ni oir, ni hablar. ¡Bastante
ha visto y ve lo que tiene delante!

A MINER

He's sitting there, sitting
on top of his acid shadow,
on his right, god, on his left, head bent,
the son. And the holy ghost drifting around in the air.
Who has fitted on this face
like a dead man's? Who has eaten from his hunger and raised
    a glass
with his thirst? Even god does not shelter him.
There you have his son, a deafmute,
and Teresa, his daughter, in a rest home or
putting it crudely, the nuthouse.
                          God-
damned mine! The heaven,
under the ground, of some mastermind somewhere.

His woman, they say, was lovely when she was a girl.
Now she's a broken umbrella. She
doesn't want to hear anything about heaven
and doesn't want to talk about it. What she has seen
and sees right there in front of her is enough.

Tierra
roída por la guerra,
triste España sin ventura,
te contemplo
una mañana de octubre,
el cielo
es de acero oxidado, el primer frío
guillotina las hojas amarillas,
patria
de mi vivir errante,
rojas colinas
de Ciudad Real,
fina niebla de Vigo,
puente
sobre el Ter, olivos alineados
junto al azul de Tarragona,
tierra
arada duramente,
todos te deben llorar,
nosotros
abrimos los brazos a la vida,
sabemos
que otro otoño vendrá, dorado y grávido,
bello como un tractor entre los trigos.

FALL

Land
gnawed by war,
unfortunate sad Spain,
I examine you
one morning in October,
the sky
is rusted steel, the first chill
guillotines the yellow leaves,
country
my life has drifted in,
red hills
of Ciudad Real,
fine mist of Vigo,
bridge
over the Ter, olive trees lined up
next to Tarragona's blue,
land
worked with difficulty,
everyone should weep for you,
we
open our arms to life,
we know
another fall will come, heavy with gold,
beautiful as a tractor in the wheat.

Hojas de Madrid

(Leaves of Madrid)

Mi casa, por desgracia, es una casa,
un calcetín colgando de un alambre,
donde escribí mis libros más sombríos
y me viré hacia la vida, a dios gracias.
Esta casa, compañero, esta casa
está sentada siempre, está sentada,
y hace frío en verano y en el invierno hace calor
(que te crees tú eso),
y yo he regresado, camarada, unos días
a recoger mis libros, mis discos, mis contratos
y he encontrado a mi madre en el pasillo
y a mi hermana en la sala,
y a mí mismo leyendo en un rincón,
comprende, compañero, que han sucedido largos días
y anchas noches, camarada, desde entonces.
Qué hacer, si he visto el mundo desde arriba
y las nubes también desde arriba,
y di la vuelta alrededor de un niño
de Pinar del Río,
y era muy distinto
a los niños de España y a los tíos de París,
ha ocurrido algo
en algunos lugares de la tierra,
compañero,
camarada, mi casa por desgracia sigue igual,
no sigue igual,
hay más discos, compañero,
más serenidad, camarada,
y más amor en voz baja, y son las siete.

SEVEN

My house, unfortunately, is a house,
a sock hanging from a line,
there I've written my saddest books,
and turned my face toward life, thank god.
This house, my friend, this house
is always sitting there, it just sits,
and in summer it gets chilly, and hot in winter,
(I suppose you believe that),
and I have come back, comrade, for a few days
to pick up my books, my records, my contracts
and I found my mother in the hall
and my sister in the living room
and myself reading in a corner,
friend, you have to understand, long days have gone by
and slow nights, comrade, since then.
What can I do, when I've seen the world from above
and even the clouds from above,
and I walked once around a small boy
in Pinar del Río,
and he was so different
from Spanish children or the wiseguys of Paris,
something has been going on
in certain spots on this planet,
friend,
unfortunately, comrade, my house is still the same,
it's not the same,
it contains more records, my friend,
and more peace and quiet, comrade,
and more love spoken in whispers, and it's seven now.

from

Mientras

(In the Meantime, 1970)

el lápiz con que tracé aquella carta a los dioses está
gastado, romo, mordisqueado

La cocina es lo más surrealista de la casa.
(Claro que me refiero a las cocinas con fogón de carbón.)
Una bombilla amarilla ilumina la dostoievskiana cocina.
Noches de invierno, con lluvia, frío o viento o granizo, y las
escuálidas gotas chorreando por la cal.
Yo he residido largamente en la tierra, esto es: sobre las
lívidas baldosas de la cocina.
He escrito muchos poemas en la cocina
y, por poco, casi he rezado en la cocina.
El mes de febrero es elegido con fruición por todas las
cocinas de provincias.
Mi cocina en Hurtado de Amézaga 36, contribuyó poderosa-
mente a la evolución de mi ideología.
(Hoy recuerdo aquella cocina como un santuario, algo así
como Fátima con carbonilla.)
Sentado en la banqueta de madera, sobre la mesa de pintado
pino melancólica luz lanza un quinqué,
según atestigua Espronceda.
Gran poeta el intrépido Espronceda.
Interesante muchacha la Teresa, que se ganó un apasionado
camafeo de octavas reales
que no se las salta un torero.
Espronceda poeta social de las cocinas y de las barricadas.
Bravo Espronceda, delicada media verónica de Gustavo
Adolfo Bécquer.
Dios mío, qué solos se quedan los muertos.
Un muerto en la cocina es algo perfectamente serio.

the pencil with which I wrote that letter to the gods is
worn down, dull, chewed up

The kitchen is the most surrealist thing in the house.
(I'm talking about kitchens with a coal range, of course.)
A yellow bulb lights up the Dostoevskian kitchen.
Winter nights, with rain, cold or wind or hail, and the
squalid drops rolling down the whitewash.
I have lived on the earth a long time, that is, on the dis-
colored kitchen tiles.
I've written many poems in the kitchen
and I almost, not quite, prayed in the kitchen.
In the country, all the kitchens are happy to pick February
as their month.
My kitchen over on 36 Hurtado de Amézaga contributed
strongly to the evolution of my thought.
(Today I think back on that kitchen as a holy place, a kind of
Fatima with soot.)
When you sit on the wooden bench, a student lamp throws a
melancholy light on the painted pine table,
we have Espronceda's word for it.
Brave Espronceda, great poet.
And that Teresa, an interesting girl, she won herself a
love-struck cameo of eight lines
that no bullfighter can leap over.
Espronceda, socially conscious poet of kitchens and rev-
olutions.
Gutsy Espronceda, delicate half veronica of Gustavo Adolfo
Becquer.
My God, the dead are so alone.
A dead man in the kitchen is a very serious thing.

O NOS SALVAMOS TODOS,
O QUE SE HUNDAN ELLOS

claro, la sociedad de consumo es la
que consume a la sociedad

Cuando se tiene el cuerpo tan cansado y dolorido,
y existe la falta de dinero, de libertad, de amor y de cara-
    melos;
cuando se vive en Madrid sin decidirse a vivir invariable-
    mente en Madrid o en los Dardanelos,
e involuntariamente se rima
y se recuerda que jamás se me hubiera ocurrido en otros
    tiempos una rima tan espontánea y elástica como
e s t a ,
y el cuerpo continúa golpeándome con los huesos,
y ya está:
        es el momento de comprender la vida en toda la exten-
            sión del sufrimiento,
la vida de Carlos V,
la vida de Romeo y Julieta,
la vida de Carlos Marx,
la vida de Sancho Panza,
la vida de Carlos Gardel
y la muerte del Che Guevara.

Porque comprender la vida en sus infinitas e idénticas
    variantes,
por ejemplo, la vida de un servidor de ustedes sabiendo a
    ciencia cierta que muy pocos de ustedes son capaces de
    comprender el más insignificante de mis actos,

EITHER WE'RE ALL GOING TO BE SAVED,
OR ELSE LET THEM SINK

the consumer society is, of course,
the one that consumes society

When your body is sore and dog-tired
and there's very little money or freedom or love or caramels
and you live in Madrid and can't decide to stay in Madrid
for good or go to the Dardanelles,
and you rhyme without trying to
and you remember that at one time I would never have come
up with a rhyme as easy and flabby as
t h i s ,
when my body keeps on using my bones to beat me,
then that's it:
it's time to understand life and everything that *suffering*
takes in,
the life of Charles V,
the life of Romeo and Juliet,
the life of Karl Marx,
the life of Sancho Panza,
the life of Carlos Gardel
and the death of Che Guevara.

Because to understand life in its infinite and identical
variations,
for example, the life of yours truly, knowing beyond a doubt
that very few of you are likely to understand even my
tiniest act,

y que, a su vez, el acto fundamental de mi vida tal vez sólo
    uno o dos de los mencionados ustedes sean dignos de
    recibirlo,
es decir, comprendiendo la magnitud de vuestro egoísmo y la
    indefensión de mi entrega;
volviendo a añadir el dolor que en este momento baja por
    mis espaldas,
escribo tan gratuitamente como a mis trece años,
sabiendo quién soy,
conociéndome perfectamente,
diferenciándome como el agua del vino de Carlos V, Romeo y
    Julieta y demás descendientes,
y continuando en Madrid por el simple hecho de continuar en
    Madrid y la relativa necesidad de apagar la nostalgia
y sin más efecto que mi presencia tan útil e inútil en mi
    propia tierra,
donde repartí unos trozos de viva voz incrustada en tres
    o cuatro trepidantes libros
que, realmente, ya no existen pues fueron vividos hasta
la saciedad y trabajados en horas extranjeras,
todo lo cual
me obliga en este momento a ventilar un poco la habitación
    y a volver a solicitar un insignificante caramelo
y unos versos
que hablen del valle de mi infancia, la madre de mi madurez
    y la mujer de mi orfandad,
diciendo:
      Respondo de las torturas,
      no con mi firma sino con mi vida.
      Apoyo
      la nube más débil de Orozco,

and that, in turn, maybe only one or two of you I've just
      mentioned will be worthy of receiving the fundamental
      act of my life,
I mean, bearing in mind your tremendous egoes and the
      helpless way in which I offer myself;
bringing up again the pain creeping down my back right now,
I write as gratuitously as I did at thirteen,
knowing who I am,
understanding myself perfectly,
seeing that I am as different from Charles V, Romeo and
      Juliet and the other grandsons as wine is from water,
and staying on in Madrid for something as simple as staying
      in Madrid and because of the general need to quench my
      homesickness
and without any more effect than my presence, so useful and
      useless in my own part of the country,
where I handed out a few pieces of living voice encrusted in
      three or four jarring books
that really don't exist anymore, they were lived out
all the way and worked out on foreign time,
all of this
forces me right now to air out my room a little and ask again
      for a caramel that doesn't mean anything,
and some lines
that will speak of the valley of my childhood, the mother of
      my adulthood, and the wife of my orphanhood,
saying:

      I answer for the tortures,
      not with my signature but with my life.
      I support
      the faintest cloud over Orozco,

el cansino caminar
de mi madre,
y la destrozada sonrisa
sudeste,
reuniendo en un solo grito
la justicia
apaleada,
el indeciso itinerario de la niebla
y la ingravidez del vientre materno,
no digáis
que enmudeció la elvira agotado su tesoro,
seamos serios
hasta el final.

¿Se entiende bien mi firma? Seguiré en Madrid o repartiré
caramelos
en otro lugar en que me decida a vivir, a variar, a rimar
inclusive,
repitiendo "hay pastillas, bombones, caramelos", en un
espontáneo y sabroso endecasílabo?
No. Yo no aguanto Madrid.
Prefiero fumar hasta tapiarme los bronquios.
A mí no me pilla
la sociedad de consumo, como hizo aquel taxi en 1927 en una
esquina de la calle del Barquillo.

my mother's
tired walk
and that shattered smile
southeast of here,
putting into one single cry
justice
beaten with clubs,
the mist's unsteady course
and the weightlessness of a mother's womb,
don't say
elvira lost her voice once her treasure was all
    spent,
let's be serious
down to the end.

Can you read my signature all right? Will I stay on in Madrid
    or give caramels away
someplace else I may decide to live in, to vary, even to rhyme,
repeating "tootsie rolls, jelly beans, gum drops, caramels,"
    in easy and delicious hendecasyllabics?
No. I can't stand Madrid.
I prefer to smoke until I block up my bronchials.
The consumer society
will never run over me, like that taxi in 1927 on a corner of
    Barquillo Street.

UNA ESPECIE DE

la paz se ha destrozado, y el cielo es
una lamentable tienda de campaña

Y si yo en vez de ir esta noche al teatro me fuese a Viet-Nam.
¿Quién escribe, quién me coge la mano? No es mía.
Nada me pertenece: ni la máscara, ni el personaje.
Y si yo esta noche

me fuese a Viet-Nam.
Un pobre diablo bebe un vaso de agua. No ocupa su localidad.
Se sienta.
Somos dos. El Norte y los Títeres. Maese Pedro se llama el
tercero, la celestina. Y si yo en vez de llamarme
Murueta Sagarminaga
me fuese y me llamasen unión unión
contra el vaso de agua, la sed, el verso libre y el deber.
El día veinticinco de junio no teníamos armas.
El día veintiséis de julio no teníamos armas.
Sólo un soldado. Y millones de proyectos, hombres, pero
carecíamos de armas.
Proyectiles en una palabra.
Aquí estoy sentado en medio de los escombros de Hue.
En mitad de la República Democrática y en mitad de la otra
misma república democrática (*sic*).
Parado ante una piedra. En pie. Terriblemente desocupado
de invasores, sintiendo los aviones bajar subir sesgar
la noche—así el tirón rasgándose la tela.
¿Qué hacéis por ahí arriba? Pobres diablos, venid
a ver la función: sentaos tras la ametralladora.

SOMETHING LIKE A

peace has been destroyed and
the sky is a pitiful tent

And what if instead of going to the theater this evening I
    went off to Vietnam.
Who is writing, who is holding my hand? It is not mine.
Nothing is mine. Neither the mask, nor the role.
And what if this evening
                                        I went off to Vietnam.
Some poor devil drinks a glass of water. He's not in his
    theater seat. He sits down.
That makes two of us. The North and the Puppets. Maese
    Pedro is the third one's name, the pimp. And what if
    instead of being called Murueta Sagarminaga
I went off and they called me union union
against the glass of water, thirst, free verse and duty.
On June twenty-fifth we had no weapons.
On July twenty-sixth we had no weapons.
Just a soldier. And millions of projects, and men, but we
    lacked arms.
Missiles in one word.
Here I am sitting in the middle of the rubble of Hue.
Halfway into the Democratic Republic and halfway into the
    other same democratic republic (*sic*).
Standing in front of a stone. At attention. Terribly unworried
about invaders, hearing the airplanes descending climbing
    ripping through
the night—like fabric tearing at one jerk.

Oíd. Vais a morir. No disparar, porque vais a morir de un
momento a otro. Todos.
Tirad tirad tirad tirad tirad porque de todos modos vais a
morir.

Un mínimo resplandor y el día, un día concreto, lunes
dieciocho de febrero rodea parte del cielo. Pronto os voy
a ver la cara
machacada al pie de la letra, en el lugar donde brilló el
avión. Venid,
tirad tirad tirad tirad, os queda sólo un hombre.

Una especie de verso que un perro husmea entre la basura.

What are you doing up there? Poor devils, come
and see the performance: sit behind the machine gun.
Listen. You're all going to die. Don't shoot, because you're
    going to die any minute now. All of you.
Shoot shoot shoot shoot shoot because you'll die anyhow.

A tiny glimmer and the day, a specific day, Monday February
    eighteenth circles part of the sky. I'll soon be seeing
    your face
literally pounded to bits, at the spot where the airplane
    flashed. Come on,
shoot shoot shoot shoot, you only have one more man to go.

Something like a line of poetry a dog sniffs at in the trash.

MEETING BLAS DE OTERO

(An interview with Blas de Otero by Antonio Nuñez.)

What is poetry for you? A means of transforming society? Evasion . . . ?

I prefer to talk about poems rather than poetry. In fact, poetry only exists in poems and I strongly believe that it's just one of the many things a man can make on earth. As for the idea of a poem conceived as a means of transforming society, I think poetry is intimately connected to its origins and, by the same token, the poet is bound to society from the start, because, no matter what political regime the poet lives under, and whether or not he is aware of it, society shapes him. At the same time, the poem makes its dent on society whether the poet consciously intended it or not. Now then: as far as my opinion and personal stand are concerned, one of the poem's jobs is to get through to society, keeping in mind that society is made up of men and poetry must touch these men.

As for evasion, I don't believe poetry is that, because it would be a weakness that served to sidestep problems and it would amount to a betrayal. But what I want to say is that it has to be accomplished in the poem and the poem is a work of art, and follows certain rules with certain end points. In short, its quality as art is something you can't get around.

What characteristics are central to your poetry? Do you feel that your work has evolved?

I don't like to talk about my own work, either in general, or in specific terms about any of my books, because that implies a kind of self-analysis or looking into oneself inside the work itself. Generally speaking, I am very aware of myself when I work out a poem, and yet once it's done I don't like to go back to it. But, apart from this, I agree with critics and readers who see an evolution—this word is well used because for me there has never been a scission—in my work. The content has always been man, which in *Fiercely Human Angel*, for example, had a strictly personal and subjective tone, contained in the eternal and constant themes that haunt man, such as death, and love. But even at this early stage, in *Drumroll of Conscience* and *Fiercely Human Angel*, there was a historical interest in man.

As regards form, my poems have been growing more and more direct in expression, especially aiming to eliminate rhetoric and the abuse of image and metaphor. You might call it a doubling back to simplicity, bearing in mind the difference between the simplicity of the adolescent poet or one who has not yet fully developed and that of the poet who achieves simplicity in his work through the elimination of dead-weighted elements. And speaking of form, in the sense of what shape the poem has, it can be seen from my books that I have used almost every kind and type of verse; in my early work, there is a poem called "World," from *Drumroll of Conscience*, that is entirely free verse; people now consider it one of my representative poems. Besides, in this poem, written around 1947–1948, the theme is already the historical situation at the time. This same type of poem also appears in my last published book, *All about Spain* (I am talking about the Paris and Havana editions, which are complete, because the Barcelona edition is horribly censored, with some hundred poems missing; but let me clear up a couple of things about so-called free verse. What I want to emphasize is that this kind of poem has its own strict laws, like any other poem. Chief among them are two factors so often neglected today, namely *rhythm* (determined by the internal rhythm or movement) and the *word* (after all poetry is made with words). Another point to consider: the sonnets I have written, though their outer structure follows tradition, hendecasyllables in two quartets and two tercets, I believe that often only the appearance is the same.

What themes preoccupy you?

I've already touched on some of them, but today I would say that, above all, "the theme of Spain" interests me, and the universal ones, historically speaking, most of all that of peace, an active peace, and the struggle of the so-called underdeveloped and colonized countries and those that are victims of neocolonialism.

What is the intellectual's role in the world?

Today the intellectual, perhaps more than ever before, has a great responsibility before the world, before other men, and he can fulfill this by taking a resolute stand in the social and political realm, but he must stand up first of all in his own work, whether that be a poem or a novel or a scientific work. I say this because there happen to be writers who in the sphere of action take a clear stand, but in their work this position is not reflected or else they don't even take up those problems in it.

The role of our intellectual is really inescapable, one of tremendous responsibility and, also, of a relative and positive efficacy. The role of the intellectual is to criticize and help orient, and in the near future, when we achieve the authentic democracy that we all demand, this task will be more feasible and visible.

What, in your judgment, are the main difficulties a Spanish writer runs into? Economic? The lack of freedom of expression?

These difficulties are known and suffered by all of us and, in my specific case, it should be kept in mind that I haven't been able to publish a book in Spain since 1955, because *Ancia*, which belongs to 1958, is only a re-edition of previous books, and as I've said, the Spanish edition of *All about Spain* was badly chopped up.

What about Spanish poetry right now? Do you think the "social" preoccupation of poets is at a crisis point? How do you view your place in the general panorama of Spanish poetry?

Just yesterday, I read an interview with Carlos Sahagun, the young poet, in a Madrid newspaper, in which he answered this question by saying that the so-called social poetry has not lost its authentic value, "as though it were just another fashion, equally capable of being launched or withdrawn from the market, anytime." Social poetry has been abandoned by those who used it as a fashion, but not by those who recognized it as a need of their own spirit and their time. Sahagun also spoke, and here he hit the nail on the head, about whether social poetry is or is not for the masses. As you know, in 1949 I had what some consider the gall to put the dedication "To the immense majority" at the front of *Fiercely Human Angel*. In the last book I published, *All about Spain*, there's a poem called "C. L. I. M." that stands for "Con la inmensa mayoria" ("With the Immense Majority"). In this poem I insert an epigraph that says: "In the conditions of *our hemisphere* poetry is for the majority not because of the number of its readers, but because of its theme." This means that a book of poems that touches on the social and political problems of this immense majority, that takes up its stand with it, is *per se* a book for that majority, whether it is later read by three hundred or three hundred thousand people, for this second aspect doesn't depend on what is fundamental in the poems themselves, but on extraliterary causes. Conversely, there are many books that run to editions of hundreds of thousands and obviously, they are not for the majority, in the honest sense of the word, but, we might say, inframajoritarian. Now then, when a book of poems embodies the position I've previously described and if it also contains— I repeat and underline—real poetic merit, this kind of book is for the immense majority, although of course this expression doesn't mean that everyone will read it, but we are talking of a circle of readers or of the range of literature.

What Spanish authors do you feel closest to?

In poetry, to Fray Luis de Leon, the *Romancero* and the traditional and popular *Cancionero*. In addition, I feel that the Peruvian Cesar Vallejo and the Turkish poet Nazim Hikmet are two of the four or five most important poets of this century.

Do you think poetic creation is limited by political partisanship, or do you consider this inacceptable?

Taking sides is a question of making an internal decision. It means that the poet feels certain things very strongly and deeply: with this to go on, his creation is free and spontaneous, although the result of the poem may seem to some stuffed shirts a pamphlet, or prescribed, or an occasional poem. What is of interest, I repeat, is the internal condition of the poet as a man. So much so, that if a poet writes a poem, let's say in defense of the Vietnamese people, because this tragedy affects him profoundly, it is more than anything a poem of love.

Has Spanish society come to realize what a poet is, or is he still considered a kind of oddball, marginal, not serious?

Unfortunately things haven't changed much, but this is due for the most part to causes outside literature, and in order to change all this we have to begin by radically modifying certain structures, that would bring *a posteriori* a change in man's mental attitude about the function of culture, and so on.

Tell us about your last two books.

One of them puts together poems under the general title *Poetry and History*, that I hope will be published in Spain and read by the largest possible number of readers. It's a book that came out of extended visits to several socialist countries in the years since 1960. One part of the book is called "With Cuba." The other is a book of prose pieces, called *Imagined and True Stories* that I don't think can be fitted into any set literary genre. They're not prose poems. They are really some ninety prose pieces, whose form is determined by the content, that sometimes resemble a kind of essay and at others a kind of narrative, or recollection, or travel piece. It's my hope that this book will appear in Spain.

This interview, which has been slightly abbreviated, appeared in the literary review Insula, *no. 259, June 1968. Since then, Blas de Otero has published three books in Spain: in 1969, an anthology of poems taken from all of his previous books, including some from books printed abroad, with new poems and prose pieces;* Imagined and True Stories, *in 1970; and that same year,* In the Meantime, *his first collection of new poems published in Spain since 1955, if we except the chopped-up edition of* All about Spain, *which Otero discounts in the interview.*—Editor's note.

BOOKS BY BLAS DE OTERO

Blas de Otero's books include three very slim first volumes: *Cuatro poemas* (*Four Poems*), ed. Arbor, no. 6, Pamplona, 1941; *Cántico espiritual* (*Spiritual Song*), ed. Cuadernos del grupo Alea, San Sebastián, 1942; and *Poesías en Burgos* (*Poems in Burgos*), ed. Escorial, no. 34, 1943. His most important books of poems are *Angel fieramente humano* (*Fiercely Human Angel*), Madrid, 1950; *Redoble de conciencia* (*Drumroll of Conscience*), Barcelona, 1951; *Pido la paz y la palabra* (*I Ask for Peace and the Right to Speak*), ed. Cantalapiedra, Torrelavega y Santander, 1955; *Ancia* (A title made up with the first syllable of *Angel fieramente humano* and the last syllable of *Redoble de conciencia*. It was a re-edition of these two books, with forty-eight additional poems written at the same time as the poems in those books but never printed), Barcelona, 1958; *En castellano* (*In Plain Words*), ed. as *Parler clair* by Pierre Seghers, Paris, 1959, in a bilingual edition; *Esto no es un libro* (*This Is Not a Book*), ed. University of Puerto Rico, 1963; *Que trata de España* (*All about Spain*), ed. Ruedo Ibérico, Paris, 1964; and *Mientras* (*In the Meantime*), ed. Javalambre, Zaragoza, 1970. His first book of prose, from which the three pieces included here were taken, *Historias fingidas y verdaderas* (*Imagined and True Stories*), ed. Alfaguara, Madrid-Barcelona, was published in 1970.